BEARS
OF ALASKA
in life & legend

JEFF RENNICKE

with contributions by
Dr. Charles Schwartz
Harry V. Reynolds
Steven C. Amstrup

ROBERTS RINEHART, INC. PUBLISHERS
BOULDER, COLORADO
in cooperation with
THE ALASKA NATURAL HISTORY ASSOCIATION
ANCHORAGE, ALASKA

For my teacher, Bernard Hupperts,

and, for all the silent landscapes
which have lost the bears,
an emptiness without echo.

Copyright © 1987 by Christina Watkins
Published by Roberts Rinehart, Inc. Publishers
Post Office Box 3161 Boulder, Colorado 80303
in cooperation with Alaska Natural History
    Association
International Standard Book Number
    0-911797-29-7
Library of Congress Catalog Card Number
    86-64042
Printed in Hong Kong through Interprint,
    San Francisco
Designed and Produced by Christina Watkins

CONTENTS

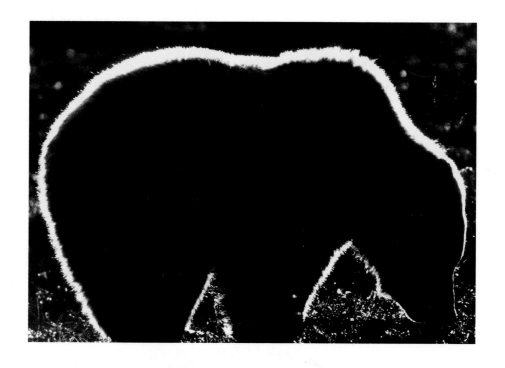

ALASKA: A LANDSCAPE FOR BEARS

"It is difficult to envision what the popular image of Alaska might be, or how Alaskans would see themselves, or what would happen to their unique sense of place, if there were no more bears in the state."

Morgan Sherwood
Big Game in Alaska

ARCTIC WINTER. The Kenai Peninsula. There is a cold here so pure it turns the sky to brittle blue and the air in your lungs to icy slivers. December, and the sun is low and cold and wraps the forest in light the color of week-old ice. No motion but our own. No tracks but those of our snowshoes. No sound, just a silence as soft and sure as the flight of a snowy owl.

Dr. Charles Schwartz and his research team track bears to their dens in this winter woods each year as a part of the ongoing studies of the Alaska Department of Fish and Game. There are no bears in sight here, no tracks or sign, just the rhythmic signal from the radio telemetry equipment Schwartz carries in his pack. Deep beneath the drifts of snow and ice of this place black bears and grizzlies lay firm in the grasp of the long winter's sleep.

Even though there are no tracks, this is the place that best begins an understanding of Alaskan bears. In bear country a presence remains on the landscape as certainly as if the weight of their steps had formed these frozen lakes and the hot steam of their breath had created the clouds overhead. There are Eskimo stories that say it happened just this way; and standing in such a winter woods listening to the metallic beeping of the radio signal sounding like a faint, far off heartbeat, it is difficult not to see it so. The bear, even in the deepest Arctic winter, is upon the landscape.

No other North American mammal commands this powerful a presence. It has been felt by trappers, prospectors and mountain men, described by poets and storytellers around late-night campfires, everyone who has been in bear country. There is an endlessness to the skies, a depth to the shadows that comes with the realization of a place as "bear country." Perhaps it is just that the bear inhabits only the pristine and most remote places that have a wildness all their own. Perhaps it is the late-night bear stories. Whatever the reason, a place seems wilder with bear tracks embroidering its riverbanks. And, no matter what creatures share the landscape—wolf, moose, caribou— it will, as long as the bears remain, be bear country.

But, in places outside of Alaska the bear populations are falling. Pushed by

the remnants of the kind of steel-jawed hatred that resulted in the predator control programs of the early part of the century, the laying of poison-laced meat traps, the shotgun barrels of stockmen and government hunters and, more than anything else, the full-scale war on their habitat by development, the bears range over a much smaller part of the North American landscape than just a century ago.

There will soon come a time when living memory will not recall the sight of a grizzly among the snowfields of the High Sierras in California, or the days when the Colorado Rockies were home to grizzlies. It will not be long before no one can remember summers where the polar bears came to St. Matthews Island off the northwestern Alaska coast. Still, in places if one looks closely, bends back the grasses, there may yet be faint trails where the bears for so many seasons walked; there may be unmistakable and easily followed trails even a generation after the last bear has passed, but the bears themselves are gone.

As the bears disappeared, a few began to realize that when a place loses its bears more has passed from the landscape than just an animal. There is a stillness to such a place—an emptiness without echo. More than any other animal the bear can bring life to the wild places. There is a grace to the lines of a hillside, a bluer tint to the skies, a clarity to bear country. And, there is an aching hollowness to a place where the bears have been killed out. The land goes silent.

Only one animal can inspire such extremes. Bears are perceived as creatures of extreme: cute and cuddly or blood-thirsty killers. It is a reputation which has both its beginnings and its end in the human mind, yet there is no denying the power of the animal over the human experience. Realization of this power and the growing understanding of its importance to the human wilderness experience is coming late, too late for the bears in some areas. But as it comes, interest is turning to those few places left on the maps that can still be legitimately called "bear country."

Alaska is bear country. Nowhere are the tracks deeper or more fresh. It is a landscape for bears. A major reason it remains so is its size and remoteness and the extremes of its climate, but it is more than that. One way to begin to understand this is to fly over a part of the state in a small plane. It is a land unbroken. The lines are the lines of a mountain range rising out of an inlet, the ripped edge of treeline, the tangle of rivers turning quiet oxbows.

From the window of a plane, it seems a formidable land with its strengths in space and depth and distance—a land, more than most, bound only by its horizons. Once on the ground, however, on foot, the scene begins to change. The spaciousness remains, but with your eyes at ground level subtle threads become apparent. With its awesome swings in climate from endless summer daylight to the steel-hard cold of winter comes a short growing season and so a slow ability to heal for the land. The scars of a bulldozer passing even once

It is said,
if a pine needle falls
in the forest,
the eagle will see it,
the deer will hear it,
and the bear will catch
its scent.

over the tundra may disrupt the pattern of permafrost and leave visible tracks that will take decades to vanish. This is a strong land knitted together in a fragile balance.

Outside of Alaska, there is a misconception of what is really here, the old joke of holding up a blank white paper and calling it a picture of Alaska in winter. To many, Alaska is seen as one unbroken and unbreakable wilderness. This is a false and dangerous notion. Alaska is susceptible to the same pressures and abuses which have tipped the ecological scales in other parts of the continent, perhaps even more susceptible with its climate. Despite its awe-inspiring breadth, or perhaps because of it, the frailty of the land is astonishing.

The first feeling of the visitor to Alaska is one of complexity. Then of uniqueness. Alaska is a land of superlatives, one-of-a-kinds. There are glaciers as big as entire northeastern states; coastlines which meander for more unbroken miles than all the shorelines of the lower forty-eight states; endless mountain ranges climaxing at the 20,329-foot summit of "the Great One," Denali. It is a big land, as the sourdough reminded the boastful Texan by threatening to cut it in half and make Texas only the third biggest state.

There is a similar feeling about the bears here. Nowhere else in the United States do all three species of North American bear—the black bear *(Ursus americanus)*, the grizzly *(Ursus arctos)*, and the polar bear *(Ursus maritimus)*—occur within the boundaries of a single state. This state is, in every sense, bear country.

With the broad ranges and distributions of the three bear species, there are few places in Alaska which cannot be classified as bear country. Black bears, the most common and widespread of the species, range almost everywhere there are trees. Grizzlies and brown bears, today considered to be one species, can be found from the coastal areas to deep within the interior. Polar bears, which are more creatures of the ice than of the land, are found both off the north and northwestern shores. Wherever you are standing in Alaska, you are never far from a bear. Bears, in Alaska, are never far from your thoughts.

Bears tred deeply in the human mind. The tracks of all three species can be traced across the art, legend, dance and philosophies of Native cultures. The Natives of Alaska were, and in some cases still are, people of the land, taking both their life and their way of life from their surroundings. Modern cultures elsewhere, driven far from these roots, often find it difficult to appreciate what a force an animal like a bear can be both on the physical landscape and the landscape of the mind. For cultures which have shared the countryside with the bears for countless generations, that power was apparent. It was a power that went beyond the obvious physical strengths and touched on poetry.

Perhaps as much as natural habitats for bears have been altered in places, the political, social and economic habitat for Alaskan Native peoples have

changed too in the last decades. Few villages follow the traditional subsistence lifestyle in modern times. Modernization has brought staggering changes to these people and their traditions. Sadly, few of the tales recounted in these pages are heard any longer outside the confines of literature. Many were never meant to be read, only to be heard across the crackling of an autumn hunter's campfire. Most of the rituals described here have fallen out of use. They are not given as some sentimental reminiscence; they are given with a sense of recognition for another way than our own of viewing the animal and for their lingering effect on the way we perceive bears today. There is more, much more, that remains untold. Stories, in times past, were considered the possession of the teller and many have gone to the grave with that teller. Alaska, particularly northern Alaska, was not surveyed by anthropologists until the late 1850s, and by that time much had already been lost. There is, too, a place for silence.

Despite the abundance of spring and the protection of the sow, mortality is high in cubs of all bear species emerging from the winter den (left).

Then, there is another new and very exciting aspect of bears to be considered: scientific research. Much of the scientific data presented within these pages was unknown a decade ago. Some of it is still theoretical. Some of the legends told are as old as the sheen on the river-worn rocks. The combination can bring us closer to an understanding of the animal than was possible ever before.

Radio telemetry has thrown light into the darkness of the winter den and begun to unravel the mysteries of the long winter's sleep. New immobilization techniques have brought us closer to the innermost workings of the bear than ever before. Satellite photography has shown us a new view of habitat types. A bear, both old and new, is emerging.

Of all the bear species, the polar bear is the least understood, yet new research techniques such as radio-telemetry and immobilization are helping scientists to gather information which will be vital to the management of the species throughout the Arctic.

The work of these scientists is bringing forth a view of the animal never before considered and at the same time verifying some "myths" handed down through the centuries.

Scientists have discovered that the bear is not nearly so aggressive as popularly portrayed in sporting literature. A close look at the mythologies of Native cultures could have told us that years ago. New observations prove— contrary to what some would like to believe—that bears do sometimes kill for reasons other than hunger and do kill and devour others of their own species. Legend has known this for centuries.

Science is shooting down some myths as well. Research has shown that bears do not technically "hibernate." Winter activity of bears is more subtle and evolved.

All in all, science is adding a new and valuable layer to our understanding of the bear world. When taken as a complement to the realm of myth and legend and not completely separate from them, new horizons of knowledge become visible.

If all of this is proving one thing, it is the need for an acknowledgment of the variability within a species, even within an individual bear. One long-time bear hunting guide I spoke with already understood this. When I asked him about grizzlies, he replied "Which one?"

It is not a question to be taken lightly. The real bear is as complex as the landscape and as fluid as the flow of a river. It is a combination of the bear shown to us by research and the animal which roams the legends. Bears are a unique combination of power and poetry found nowhere else in the animal kingdom. That is apparent the first time you see a bear in the wild.

Harold McCracken called the sight of a bear in the wild "the climax of a thousand dreams and ten years of hoping." It often happens suddenly. A bear crosses the shallows of the creek below camp. The sight of it will burn in your memory. It quickens you. You will find yourself remembering things—the names of flowers, the color of the sky at that moment—that otherwise would have gone unnoticed. You recall the tilt of its head, its stance, and later find that your heart raced and your fists remained clenched long after the bear vanished over the ridge. That is part of the power.

Yet, it is all too conceivable in today's world with its distancing from the wild places that many will never see the "climax of a thousand dreams" by coming upon a bear in its natural habitat. Theirs will be the bear of photography and literature. There is a sadness in such a view of life that shivers one like a cold wind. For those, there remains the comfort of knowing that such an animal exists somewhere and that somewhere the tracks are deep and fresh.

In whatever form, the bear leaves its mark on all that it touches—both landscapes and cultures—and takes with it more than it leaves. Bears are elusive creatures. There are those who have spent years in wild places and seen only tracks or quick glimpses of shadows moving just out of sight. Therefore, it is only a glimpse that we can hope for here. No legend, no memory, no scientific paper, no book can be asked to capture all that makes up the animal. Much is uncapturable. That is part of the poetry.

What most needs to be captured is the correct balance of knowledge and awe. We need, for the survival of the species, to understand the habits and habitat of the bear. Scientists must uncover these secrets for it is a frightening fact that if there are to be bears on this continent it will be only because of a conscious human choice.

A part of making that choice is in the recognition of the place for such an animal. We need not understand why the mountains seem to rise higher and clearer in bear country or what that feeling is that sweeps over us like a chill when we lean over fresh bear tracks along the river; we need only acknowledge the existence of such magic and its place in our lives.

With that combination, if it is not beyond our grasp, the full hollowness left by the extinction of such a magnificent animal as the bear may never be known. This land, Alaska, may never go silent.

J.R.
Kenai Peninsula, Alaska

BLACK BEAR
OF SHADOW & LIGHT

THERE ARE PLACES in the forest where the light seems webbed, where shadows take on a motion of their own. There, the sunlight comes in waves with the wind. These places are not in the deep woods, thick with itself, but out near the edges where the trees grow straight and more than an arm's reach apart; where the wind blows easily and the sunlight is straight as meadow grass. This is where you'll find the black bear.

The black bear is a creature of the forest edge. For a million years black bears, and for millions of years before that their ancestors, have lived in the shadows of the forest and the sunlight of small clearings. The years have left their mark.

Dark as a moonless sky, cinnamon, brown as silt-laden streams, its coat is the colors of the forest. It can move, almost silent, through a stand of alderbrush that would tangle the wind; or crouch still as stone in the tall grass while a cow moose with calf tests the wind.

Omnivorous, it takes what the forest gives: green sprouts, buds, winterkill in the spring; moose calves, roots, grass, insects in the summer; berries, seeds, fruit and fish in the fall.

Daylight finds it resting in the thickets or ambling downstream along the creek searching for trout stranded by the dryspell. Darkness is for foraging in the undergrowth or following the scent of moose over the ridge.

Spring is for cubs, summer for mating, fall for laying on the fat in the high berry patches. Winter is for denning beneath a tangle of roots in a fallen cottonwood or in a hole scratched into a south-facing slope. Spring, it begins again.

This is the cycle which has been turning over for a million years, spring to winter, forming the black bear into the most numerous and widespread bear in North America. These years of shadow and light have left deep marks on the bear and its behavior; marks which can be seen in its form, its track and in the human mind.

As early as 1607, the black bear was called "the lesser" of the North American bear species. In the human mind, the immense form of a grizzly

"The black bear . . . is the spirit of the wilderness."

Barbara Ford
The Black Bear

13

outlined against the sunset will always call up separate and deeper emotions. But fear is a single and straightforward emotion. The black bear has an interest which goes beyond fear and touches on survival and on questions about the role of the environment in the shaping of an animal. The black bear is a different animal, hardly "the lesser", with strengths and traits and legends all its own. And the reasons go deeper than tracks in the spring mud.

EVOLUTION: THE ANCIENT STEP. All which we see as the black bear, in reality and in the human mind, began with a single, ancient step: a step the black bear didn't take.

All the North American bear species had their ancestral beginnings in the forest. Common bloodline between them broke nearly a million years ago when what was to become the modern-day grizzly, and later form the polar bear branch, stepped out of the shadowy forest and onto the sun-drenched tundra. The black bear remained in the forest and time began to form the differences which would so determine the future of the species.

Begin with the claw. Those tracks along the riverbank tell a longer story than that of a single bear, it is the story of a species. Sharper, narrower, more curved, the claw of a black bear is that of a climber. Cubs can climb from the time they emerge from the den. Adults, even with the added bulk, can climb with surprising agility, and trees, to a black bear, are places for feeding, playing and resting.

Foremost, however, trees mean safety. Cubs scamper up the nearest tree at the first sign of danger or at a signal from the sow. Adult bears, when danger approaches, can often just hide motionless in the shadows until the danger has passed, or they too can climb a tree to safety. The tendency to retreat and climb has earned the black bear a less aggressive reputation. That is sometimes a dangerous assumption, particularly when surprising a bear in the open or too near its cubs. With lightning speed, sharp claws and surprising strength, a black bear can be a formidable opponent. Yet the ability of the black bear to avoid direct conflict with the new predator on the block, Man, has played a major role in maintaining its steady populations.

The need to be able to climb as a defense tactic and the more closed-in nature of its forest habitat have also made the black bear the smallest of the North American bear species. Those who have never seen a black bear in the wild will often imagine the animal much larger than it really is. Although there have been black bears recorded at over 600 pounds and six and a half feet long, most are no bigger than large dogs and weigh less than a large man.

Smaller size and its retreat defense takes the bear a step further. These traits mean that a black bear cub is safer on its own at a much younger age than other bear species. By the time the leaves bud on its second spring, the black bear cub has been weaned, freeing the sow to mate more frequently, meaning more young can be produced in the lifespan of the bear.

All of these traits—elusiveness, greater productivity, adaptability and a less menacing image—have helped the black bear become the most numerous and widespread American bear. It is a species which fits more readily into the human concept of landscape. Most of the borderless, untouched tracts of land are gone, cut up. Yet even where habitat for such animals as grizzlies and wolves has been destroyed by development, the black bear's ability to melt like a fallen leaf into those scattered patches of woodlands left intact has given it a home. Sightings are common around highly populated areas such as Anchorage and Fairbanks where cover is still available near the city limits. One research project followed a black bear in a frequently visited city park for months without a single sighting by park goers.

The human concept of landscape has begun to mature, accepting the fact that there can be lands which stand more for the benefit of other living creatures than for human use. Perhaps it is not in time for species like the grizzly or the wolf in some areas, but the future of the black bear looks secure; a security and a future which may rest on that one step not taken nearly a million years ago.

This Eskimo shaman's mask represents the moment in which the inua *(man-spirit) of a black bear revealed itself.*

L EGENDS OF THE HUNTER AND THE HUNTED. Both Man and bears are hunters. The act of hunting such a powerful animal as the bear has built up a thick layer of legend around both the hunter and hunted. It is life and death which inspire legend and hunting was both to Man and bear.

Many of the same traits which have kept the black bear roaming the paths of the forest can be seen in the bear which roams the mythologies. But there is more, too. Man looks at the black bear and sees, more than anything, himself.

Many Arctic cultures believed that all parts of creation—rocks, rivers, storms, animals—had souls. In an environment where a flood could silt the streams and ruin the spring fishing, or a change in the path of the caribou migration could spell starvation, the connections were apparent and direct. Giving the natural world a soul meant that direct action could be taken to appease the spirits of the rivers and caribou to set the world right again.

The humanness of these spirits, given to bears as well, was reflected in the language. Bering Sea Eskimos referred to the spirit as *Inua,* or "its man." Each animal was thought to have a human-like spirit within it and that spirit would often show itself in the myths by shoving aside its muzzle to reveal a human face and by speaking in a human voice.

With the black bear there may have been more than just the belief in the *Inua* which prompted the human comparisons. Stretching to reach a limb,

15

sitting on its haunches in the sun or rearing up on its hind legs to catch a scent, the black bear can look uncannily human. The resemblance is more than just in passing.

Many of the muscle groups of the bear, particularly those of the chest and forepaws, are proportioned in much the same way as the human chest and arms. The bone structure, again in the upper body and nowhere else as closely as the paw, also resemble the human skeleton. The exactness of the match can be eerie and the likeness is most apparent and graphic in a skinned animal. Standing over a fresh kill the hunter could not have missed how hauntingly the carcass resembled the body of a stout, thick-legged man. It is an image which must have found its way into the voices of the storytellers around the campfire in the hunting camps.

Anthropologists have unearthed some of the stories told around those campfires and they show all the complexity of bear habits and behavior; from talking bears to maulings to bears marrying humans to bears helping hunters, all are common motifs in the stories. But the stories told in some camps were considered the sacred property of the teller, only to be told by that teller and taken to their grave. The stories were a part of the life and soul of a hunter, much like his spear or knife. Respect is due the possessions of a hunter.

Then, too, such stories rarely confine themselves well to paper. Some of the heart dies out with the flames of the fire. The difference between the written and oral traditions are greater than they sometimes appear. Still, enough of the stories remain to give us at least a glimpse of the bear's place in legend.

Bears were thought to be very powerful and have many human abilities.

One of these was the ability to understand human language and to be able to hear people talking from great distances. Hunters would speak softly to the bear as they stalked closer, whispering of their respect for the bear's power and their need for meat and hides against the coming of winter. Their words, often considered by anthropologists as hunting songs, would try to convince the bear to give itself to the hunter so that he and his family could eat and stay warm.

Because of the power of the bear it was thought that only the bravest of the hunters should stalk bear and some of the techniques used to gain an advantage over the powerful animal required courageous acts. Eyak hunters would circle a tracked bear, concealing themselves in the brush, until the confused bear rose on its hind legs to catch a scent. One brave warrior would then rush beneath the bear and jam a spear upright against the bear's chest. As the bear dropped to all fours again, its own weight rammed the spear through the heart.

Since the *Inua* was released only after the kill, it was after the bear was downed that many of the rituals began. The spirit could be as important, even more so, to the hunter than the animal itself. The spirit was thought to go back to a place where other souls waited to replenish the world with game. A report on the hunter's treatment of the animal could determine future hunting success; wrongdoing or disrespect could mean famine, sickness and death.

Some hunters, such as Eyak people, would quickly gouge out the eyes of the dead animal to keep it from seeing who had killed it, but this type of ritual was rare. Most hunters wanted the *Inua* to see how respectfully the carcass was handled. Chugach buried the skull facing inland. Koyukon tossed it in the water. Others erected high poles or platforms to hold the skull.

Skinning was perhaps the most ritualized aspect of bear hunting. One man, usually the one whose spear first made contact with the animal, passed his skinning knife over the carcass once . . . twice . . . three times before making the cut on the fourth pass, thus giving the *Inua* time to prepare for the entry of the knife blade.

The black bear's uncanny and sometimes eerie resemblance to a human inspired great respect in hunters who developed complex rituals to appease the bear's spirit.

The bear was then divided. Each group had a different system of dividing the meat and usable parts. Some parts were considered choice or good luck and these would usually go to the hunter whose spear first broke the skin of the bear. Other parts were more practical than magical, such as the strong and sharp shin bones which were used by many people to make excellent spearheads.

Myths about the meat and taste for it varied widely. Tlinget had taboos against the eating of the bear. These beliefs were based on the role played by the bear in Tlinget ancestry stories. Haida also believed the bear to be a link in the people's ancestry, yet had less stringent taboos. Haida hunters would go out after a bear only following a long, purifying sweat bath. If a bear was taken, only small portions of the meat were eaten out of respect for the animal.

With the power held by the bear, it was common for certain segments of the population to be forbidden from eating bear meat. Among the Eyak of southeastern Alaska where the black bear was known as *tsiyu,* a girl in puberty was not allowed meat from a bear. A boy's first bear kill was given to older relatives as a sign of good faith towards his ancestry.

Bears were difficult game to kill and so did not play as major a role in the subsistence lifestyles as other game such as caribou. The same is true in modern times. A recent subsistence harvest survey of the northwestern region of the state showed that while 14,219 caribou were taken by subsistence hunters in a single year, only 106 black bear were harvested. Still, with their belief in a never-ending supply of game, most hunters did not concern themselves with the harvest figures, only with the treatment of the kill. This lack of a conservation ideal has opened some Native cultures to criticism from outsiders, though such an accusation seems out of context in subsistence lifestyles.

Conservation, the deliberate and planned management of natural resources, is a modern concept born out of an increased knowledge of ecosystems, a growing population's demand for the resources and a sense of domination over the environment. It is a modern, western concept that could have had little place in prehistoric or early historic Native thinking. Most of the Arctic cultures did not consider themselves in a position of domination or even stewardship of the environment. As proven by their belief in animal ancestry, most believed they were a part of the landscape. They could no more control the population of caribou through management than influence the direction of the wind. Game taken was a factor of the strength of a hunter's arm and the depth of stalking skills. If caribou were scarce, other game was taken. If bear became plentiful, for whatever reason, their tracks would be seen more often and so they would be hunted more frequently.

Conservation is a term for which there are few equivalents in traditional Native languages. As their environments became influenced by other factors—guns, snowmobiles to cover more ground, oil pipelines, sport hunting, land management by outside agencies—the term has become more familiar and management techniques have found their way into many cultures of the North.

The stories of old were of hunting as it was rooted in survival. There are stories, possibly some of them true, of mass slaughters of animals and running herds of caribou off cliffs. More often though, there are stories and legends which show a kinship and respect for the natural world. Before the advent of rifles, the length of the spear and claw arranged the hunter and the hunted spatially so that they were keenly aware of each other's strengths and weaknesses. The hunts brought these out, the best and the worst of both species and each is reflected in those legends and stories that have survived through the years.

Carved wood mask with ears of black bear fur.

CEREMONIAL MASKS: THE FACES OF BELIEF. In the nomadic world of many early Alaskan cultures there was little room for a great collection of artifacts. By necessity the body became the instrument, the dance became the medium and only a carved mask was used as costume. Together these were the most vibrant displays of native creativity and thought. An outburst of belief, the relief of humor, the drama of the chase, all portrayed in the beat of a drum and the swaying of the body.

It was a dance powered by belief, not aesthetics. Many cultures did not consider the dances an artform and so with the influx of the new western religions few of the masks or the dances have been handed down. Instead of art, the dances and the masks were tools for making an offering to the spirits. Dance was a sort of group offering. A specific purpose was served by each dance and, when that purpose was forgotten, the dancing stopped.

Motivation for the dances could be friendship, entertainment, acting out a moral but most often they were rooted in survival and that meant hunting. Bears figured greatly in hunting and so figured greatly in many of the dances and masks.

Key in the dances and the preparation of the masks was the shaman, a person of particular spiritual power. It was after the description of the shaman that the dances were orchestrated and the masks fashioned. Each mask, even for the same species, was different, a recognition of the variability in animals.

In Native thought animals and their spirits were not slaves to a single form but were free to evolve with time and the circumstances. A bear mask might be a direct interpretation of its earthly form or a surrealistic portrayal of the bear's changeable spirit. Some of these assimilations of bear and bear spirit are difficult for the non-Native eye to recognize as a bear, but we look through different eyes.

A bear mask did not represent a single animal taken that year. Each was considered a link in a chain that ran from bears taken by ancestors long ago to bears that would be taken in years to come. It was the mask of a species, the spirit of an entire race of animals.

Most of the masks were carved of wood, some no larger than a finger ring held up to the eyes. Others were so large and elaborate that the dancer could only hold them up like props. Sadly, many of the dances and the masks have been lost with the replacement of Native religions with western beliefs. There is a movement afoot in places all across Alaska and the Arctic to bring back the dances as part of a cultural revival. Some feel it is too late, too much has been lost. Others feel that the spirit of the dance is like the song of a whale which is constantly changing and can be picked up at any point and resumed. Through efforts of some museums and local arts councils carvers are again carving masks. In some cases, masks collected in early surveys by museums are being copied. In others, the masks of the bear are being carved through the eyes and hands of new artists, the modern touch, a new link added to a never-ending chain.

LEGENDS OF THE LONG SLEEP. Snowing. Through the blowing snow and the fog, the tracks of the bear wind through the trees and disappear on a hillside. Behind, the storm is silently brushing the tracks with snow.

The disappearance of bears each winter and their emergence again every spring has captured the human imagination for centuries. Like the phoenix disappearing into flames, the bear's vanishing with the first snowstorms has been likened to a sort of death. And like the rising of the phoenix, its reappearance has been seen as a kind of rebirth.

That bears den in the winter has been known for perhaps thousands of years as shown by chronologies of myth and legend. Legends told that the soul of the bear left its body for epic journeys during the cold months leaving it like a kind of shell until the snows began to melt in spring.

While it was gone, the body stayed in a kind of death-like state, said the legends. Surely it must have looked that way to the few den hunters who stumbled across a wintering bear. It was a belief that lasted nearly into this century. John Ashton, in his 1890 edition of *Curious Creatures of Zoology,* maintained that the bear was "death-like" in the den "with only a few drops of blood near the heart, but none whatever in any other part of the body."

Some theorized that the male and female spent the winter in a common den for warmth, a belief perhaps spawned by the fact that cubs will spend a second winter in the den with the sow. Edward Topsell, an early zoologist, proposed such behavior only to be forced to temper the innuendos for his decorous audiences by adding "yet do they part it by division or a small ditch in their midst, neither of them touching the other."

Theories abound, but until recently there have been no viable means to conduct the research necessary to prove or refute even the wildest of the theories. The answers were buried each year with the snows.

Then came the radio collar, a device about the size of a cigarette pack fitted on the bear after it is snared in a harmless trap and sedated. With a range of several miles, the signal transmitted by this device has allowed researchers to track bears to their dens for the first time and begin to unravel the mysteries of the long sleep.

What scientists have found is that "hibernation" is not the technically correct term for the winter activity of bears (grizzlies have similar denning habits). Theirs is a state more like a deep sleep—torpor, the scientists call it. It is a state which is much more useful for the bear. With a temperature decrease of only four to five degrees celsius, only a slightly lowered metabolism and less of a heartrate reduction than true hibernation, the bear is able to spend the winter with no food or water intake nor any elimination of wastes.

An even more useful difference is the ability for a bear to be roused from torpor to protect its cubs from wolves or other predators invading its den. A hibernating animal is much more defenseless.

Radio telemetry is a relatively new and, so far, very successful technique which has taken researchers a long way towards unraveling the mysteries of the bear's life cycles. Since studies have shown that denned bears can be easily disturbed by activity around the dens such as logging and seismic work and that bears sometimes den in areas far removed from prime feeding resources or other vital habitats, knowledge of denning patterns can play an important role in habitat protection and land use decisions. That weak, far-off beeping of the radio receiver carried by researchers may be tracking the bear into

Denning

Example: Black bear, Grizzly
Temperature Decrease: 4–5° C
Heartrate: 12 beats/minute
Metabolism: down 50%
Cycle Length: No cycle
Waste Elmination: No
Food Intake: No

Hibernation

Example: Ground Squirrel, Badger
Temperature Decrease: 30–35° C
Heartrate: 2–3 beats/minute
Metabolism: down 75%
Cycle Length: 14 days
Waste Elimination: Yes
Food Intake: Yes

more than the wilds of its denning areas, it could be tracking the way into the future.

THE SURVIVAL INSTINCT. There is a thread which runs common to all wild things: a toughness to survive. The black bear has it.

In all cultures in bear country there are stories told of the power and speed of the black bear. Even those stories told on the bear as a trickster are told with obvious reverence. Most tales go a long way towards reaffirming the discoveries of modern science; that black bears are not an aggressive species. Black bears avoid conflict. They are creatures of balance. Occasionally that balance is tipped by backpackers getting too close to cubs or by the lure of easy food at campgrounds. When it is, the black bear reaches deep for that thread of survival and can be a formidable opponent.

A bad berry crop in the hills around Fairbanks in the fall of 1963 caused the black bears to be thin, hungry and on the move. A fisherman, alone on a stretch of river he fished often, heard a rustle in the bushes behind him. Before he could turn around he was knocked into the current and pulled downstream helpless as he watched "a thin-looking black bear" cleaning up his catch.

One night that same season a hunter was pulled from his tent, still zipped into his sleeping bag, and dragged fifty yards before his shouts woke his companions who shot the bear. The man was not hurt seriously. The bear was found to be extremely thin and weak.

There are more stories of campers attacked, of researchers mauled in remote areas. People have been killed by black bears. Yet in nearly every case investigated the animal was provoked, with cubs or wounded. Verified accounts of unprovoked attacks can be counted on one hand and questions remain as to the true cause of many so-called "unprovoked" incidents.

To some extent it is a matter of percentages. As the most numerous and widespread bear species and because they inhabit the territory most often used by hikers and campers, the black bear accounts for more personal injury and property damage than the other bear species combined. Yet it is the grizzly and the polar bear which are the most feared.

All bear species have at least one common trait: unpredictability. It is a trait they wear like their fur. Dennis Branham, a master guide who has been involved in more than 400 bear hunts says, "I would never attempt to predict what any bear might do, brown, black, or grizzly bear." It is a sentiment echoed by all who know bears.

Above all, though, black bears are survivors and aggression is not a long-term survival trait. Legend has it that the black bear and the coyote will roam the earth long after the grizzly and the wolf have left only fading tracks.

In Medieval Europe it was thought that hibernating bears gave birth to shapeless lumps of flesh and licked them into bear cubs through the long winter nights.

Perhaps it is so. But the forest runs deep in the black bear and sometime long after the grizzly and wolf have vanished, a sow will bark her cubs up a tree at the movement of a wolf-like shadow on the forest edge, and an old male along the creek will rise up on its hind legs to test the wind—find no grizzly scent—and staying near the trees, move on downstream.

Taking on the hues of its forest habitat, the color phases of the black bear range from jet black to light brown to a bleached blonde from the sun to the blue-tint of glaciers bears found in the southwestern part of the state.

THE BLACK BEAR
Ursus americanus
by Dr. Charles Schwartz
Alaska Department of Fish and Game

Athabascans called him *ghedisla* or *sis*. Tlinget called him *s'eek*. To the sourdough he is "bruin" or "blackie." The scientist knows him as *Ursus americanus,* the American black bear.

DISTRIBUTION & RANGE   Today, the black bear ranges over three-fourths of the state of Alaska. Its distribution is closely associated with the coastal and boreal forests. There are no records of the black bear north of the Brooks Range, on the Seward Peninsula, the Kuskokwim Delta, the Alaska Peninsula south of the Branch River, the Kodiak Island group, or on the islands in southeast Alaska north of Frederick Sound.

Black bear abundance varies throughout Alaska and is keyed to habitat quality. Areas of known concentration occur on the Kenai Peninsula, Prince William Sound and Prince of Wales Island. In these areas, densities range from 30 to 100 bears per hundred square miles. Less is known about numbers and densities elsewhere in the state. Estimates range from 100 bears per one hundred square miles to as low as one bear in that same area.

Within these populations, individual bears do not wander randomly through the countryside. They remain within one area throughout their lives. Scientists define this area as "home range." Food abundance, to a certain extent, determines the size of home range. Female bears usually have a home range which varies in size from one and a half square miles to twenty-five square miles. Adult males maintain a home range almost ten times that size. This larger area increases the opportunity for a male to locate and breed with females.

SIZE & COLOR   Common conceptions about the size of black bears are often inflated. Adult male bears range from 200 to 400 pounds at their maximum weight in the fall, weighing almost twice as much as adult females. It is not uncommon for bears to lose up to thirty percent of their body weight during the denning period.

The Alaskan black bear is usually glossy black with a distinct fawn-colored muzzle; about twenty-five percent also have a small, white chest patch. Two other color phases also occur: the blue-grey glacier bear which is very rare and confined to the Gulf Coast, and the more common brown or "chocolate" phase most often occurring in southcentral and southeastern Alaska.

BREEDING HABITS   Population dynamics vary from area to area. Although it is possible to generalize, each population will have its exceptions. Females generally reach sexual maturity at three years of age and breed during mid-June or early July producing their first litter of cubs in their fourth winter. Litter sizes range from one to three cubs, with four being uncommon and two cubs the average. Cubs are born naked and blind, weighing less than a pound. By their emergence from the den in spring they will weigh eight to ten pounds and can gain up to thirty pounds by the next fall. Cubs will remain with the mother the first year and den with her that winter. Usually, by the following spring the family will split up when the female comes into heat. The mechanism which severs the family tie is not completely understood. Some speculate that the female becomes intolerant of her yearlings and chases them off. Others feel that it may be the breeding male which drives the young away. Whatever the cause, the family ties are broken when the bears are in their second summer.

Although most females breed every other year, cub production occurs on a less frequent basis. Black bears, like other bears, go through a process known as "delayed implantation." The egg, once fertilized, lies dormant in the uterus of the female for months until the proper conditions for growth exist. Then, the egg implants and the fetus begins development. Although not fully understood, it is believed that during years of poor berry production, female bears do not reach peak body condition and implantation does not occur. Consequently, there may be almost no cub production in some years. On the average, it appears that black bears usually produce cubs about two years out of five.

MORTALITY   Black bears have few natural enemies other than larger bears and man.

Size—Length 5–6 feet
Height 2–3 feet
Weight 200–400 lbs (m)
100–200 lbs. (f)
Diet—Omnivorous
Habitat—Forest/Clearing
Color—Black/Light Brown
Blue-Gray (rare)

Survival of cubs, after emergence from the winter den, can be a perilous proposition, and up to forty-five percent will die before the first snows fall the next winter. Cub mortality is highly variable among areas and depends on habitat quality, bear density, weather, and previous experience of the mother. Yearling and sub-adult mortality is also high and has been estimated to be as much as thirty percent. In areas where man and bear coexist, hunting and other human activities are a major cause of adult mortality. In more remote areas little is known about natural mortality. No doubt many bears die of old age, but there is evidence that some black bears, particularly sub-adults, are preyed upon by larger bears. Brown bear predation is one reason the distribution of black bears, which use trees for protection, is so closely tied to the forests.

FOOD HABITS   Bears probably spend more time searching for food and eating than on any other activity. Although classified as carnivores, the black bear is in reality omnivorous. During spring, horsetail, sedges, grass and other succulent forbs make up the bulk of their diet. By mid-summer, fruits of the early berry plants begin to ripen and bears consume these in great quantities. Devils club fruit is a major food item in late July and early August. By early fall, the berries such as blueberries and cranberries have ripened and it is by consuming huge quantities of these that the black bear gains much of its fall weight.

Animal matter does not constitute a major portion of the diet but black bears do eat salmon along many of the coastal streams. Insects, primarily those found in abundance such as ants and hornets, are eaten whenever encountered. Although beekeeping is still in its infancy in Alaska, black bear damage to hives does occur.

The black bear may appear bulky and slow, but it can be a deadly predator. Studies on the Kenai Peninsula have demonstrated that the black bears kill up to thirty-five percent of the moose calves born each spring. This predation occurs from shortly after the calves are born until the first week in July. By that time most of the healthy moose calves are strong enough to evade a pursuing bear.

DENNING   By late fall, most black bears have gained considerable weight in preparation for the denning period. Prior to denning, black bears select a site, line the cavity with nesting materials and reduce their daily activities considerably. By mid-October to early November, dropping temperatures and early snows force the bears to den.

Den sites and types vary throughout Alaska. In the Interior and on the Kenai Peninsula, bears den in natural rock caves or excavate a den in the soil. Dens are often dug under wind-swept trees, at the base of live trees, or in a hillside. On the coast near Prince William Sound and throughout the southeastern part of the state where winters are commonly wet, bears often select a hollow tree for a den site.

A typical den has a single entrance with a long tunnel leading to a chamber that is lined with vegetation to form a nest. Black bears may spend up to six months in their dens. Emergence times vary from late March in coastal areas to early May in the Interior. Although there have been sightings of black bears roaming in the winter months, most bears remain in their dens until spring. Timing of emergence seems to be related to snowmelt and weather conditions.

OUTLOOK   Black bear populations are currently healthy in Alaska. Existing hunting regulations and game management programs are aimed at assuring that overharvest and exploitation do not take place. Alaska is often seen as a sparsely populated, under-used expanse of wild country but it too is experiencing growing pains. Petrochemical, hydroelectric, mineral and other developments have the potential to alter the face of the state. This alteration may impact black bear populations. Fortunately, the black bear is an adaptable creature and experience elsewhere suggests that short of persecution or habitat elimination, the black bear will always roam the Alaskan landscape.

GRIZZLY BEAR
MYTHMAKER

THIS WAS NO MYTH. The bear had been there just moments before the bows of our canoes rounded the bend in the high Arctic river and scraped to a stop on the small spit of beach. In the thick air of a three-day rain we formed a circle around the fresh tracks. Lines were sharp; the edges unbroken; the long claw marks intact even in the rain. Bear tracks.

Upstream, the river bent north and we followed the tracks, stepping where the bear had stepped, stretching in a dance-like motion to match the gait, turning where the bear had turned, until we rounded the bend and the tracks struck inland for the mountains.

The untouched track measured nine inches long and five and a half inches wide. Grizzly tracks. Though we never saw the animal that made them, the tracks were fresh in our minds at camp that night. Years later, they are still fresh.

Few animals in North America could have made those tracks. Certainly no animal lives so shrouded in myth. The grizzly is the animal which prowls the mind of anyone who has been there, in bear country. Like the quest for tall peaks and the urge to paddle wild whitewater, it is a goal for some just to see the grizzly in its own land. The feeling of seeing a bear silhouetted against a barren autumn hillside gone orange with the coming cold is, like that of summits and whitewater, one of fear, myth, fact and the unexplainable. It is, in a word, unforgettable.

Alaska is grizzly country. The bears range from the coastal waters to the border with the Yukon Territory and north above treeline. With that range there are thousands of riverbanks with the tracks of grizzly in the sand. For each track there is a myth.

Myth plays an important role in our view of grizzlies. Whether true or told just to stuff the tenderfoot, the myths and stories have both helped and hurt the bear's chances of survival in the modern world. Some have made the bear the hero of grass-roots campaigns to protect its wilderness habitat. Others have labeled it a bloodthirsty killer creating a target for the guns and poisons

"Whenever the last grizzly bear has been dead a thousand years or more, perhaps the stories that will survive about the mighty animal will put him in the category of a demi-god of the past."

Harold McCraken
The Beast That Walks Like a Man

29

of "predator control" programs.

Around the same campfire you'll hear stories of a sow teaching her cubs the joys of frolicking in a spring snowbank. And you'll hear of a lone bear stalking a tent in the half-light of an Arctic summer night. Which is the real bear? Both? Neither? The answer is as long as the years the grizzly has roamed the earth and as complex as human emotions.

BEARS OF THE INLAND, BEARS OF THE COAST. The question of what a grizzly is has a second meaning. A battle has raged for years in hunting camps and scientific journals over the differences between the coastal brown bear and the inland grizzly.

Andrew Simon, a respected Alaskan guide, once said that he "could not distinguish the difference between a grizzly and a brown bear, of the same size, if they were walking side by side." Others have said that what was classically called a "brown bear" was larger, darker of coat and lacked the pronounced guardhairs of the inland bear.

Because of increasing pressure by sportsmen the famous Boone and Crocket Club, official record-keeper for North American game, drew the line by using a map. In 1963 it became official club policy that any bear taken within 85 miles of the coast would be considered a brown bear. Further inland, it would be a grizzly.

The line was not scientific, nor was it meant to be. In scientific circles a different criteria was being sought. For many years all coastal bears wore the tag *Ursus middendorffi,* which designated it as a separate species from *Ursus arctos horribilis,* other grizzlies. The distinction was the result of a curious scientific delineation. In the world of taxonomy there are but two kinds of classifiers: lumpers and splitters. The leading taxonomist of the early 1900s, C. Hart Merriam, was a splitter. A monograph published by Merriam in 1918 listed no less than eighty-six species and subspecies of bears in North America. Writers like Frank Dufresne followed the scientific lead and popularized the system. In his 1946 edition of Alaska's Animals and Fishes, Dufresne lists thirty species of grizzly, four of black bear and one for polar bear in Alaska alone. The system was so controversial among scientists that one taxonomist quipped, "Under such a system, twin bear cubs could be of different species."

The scientific conclusion took a step towards acceptance on July 26, 1962 when a paper published by Dr. Robert L. Rausch finally gave the brown bear a scientific home. After long studies, Rausch concluded that "formal recognition of segments of intergrading populations of brown bear at the subspecific level is not justified." Simply put, there was no need for such a complicated system of classification. The brown bear was a grizzly.

Today, all the grizzlies roam under the banner *Ursus arctos.* Still, the

An observant tracker, looking at a print in the mud near an Arctic river, could tell not only the species but the individual bear. Plaster casts made on hundreds of grizzly tracks show that the wrinkles and general formation of the pad leave patterns in the track as individual as the human fingerprint.

controversy is not yet put to rest since the bears of Kodiak Island still wear a subspecific name, *middendorffi*. With the human penchant for categorizing the battle will simmer on, though in the end it may be enough to say simply "grizzly."

IMAGES IN WOOD. Rising over the misty coastal forests, there is perhaps no more dramatic expression of Native thought in the world of art than the totem pole. Its size, workmanship, the striking colors, all command the eye. And more, the imagination. Coming across a totem pole, particularly in the place it was carved and meant to stand, is to come face-to-face with another culture. Totem poles were the lives of people carved in wood.

The most prominent figure on a pole was usually the crest. One of the most sought-after crest designs was that of the grizzly. Respected for its strength and intelligence, the grizzly crest was a sign of great honor. For a woman to be the recipient of the grizzly crest meant becoming a skilled housekeeper and a fertile wife; to the man it meant hunting skill and endurance. So powerful was the crest that the holder would sometimes go into a crazed frenzy upon receiving it, exhausting himself until cleansed. This display of power is portrayed on many totem poles by the bear's tongue being extended from its mouth.

There are many common motifs that grace totem poles from region to region, yet a pole cannot be read in the common sense of the word. One cannot start at the top and read chronologically down the events. Characters on a pole are connected only in the sense that events in a person's life are connected. The poles traced history, gave lineage, and could even indicate social status. It was a language that went beyond the confines of the written or spoken word.

The totem pole as an artform was most prevalent along coastal areas where tree growth was plentiful. These are also the areas where rain and dampness decompose artifacts quickly. There are few totem poles which stand today in their original places. A few have been preserved in museum collections but these, like an animal in a zoo, have lost much of their wonder and meaning by being taken out of context. Totem poles were connected to the land by more than the soil they stood in; they were the roots of human history and thought. In the preservation of the poles we can get a glimpse through the carver's eyes, enough for a short paragraph in a book. Yet the true and full landscape of that thought, with all its intricacies, cannot be hoped for. There are just some voices we will never hear.

Haida totem pole with bear figure second from top.

MYTHMAKER. Grizzlies are feared by some; respected by most; and for those who have lived with the bear on its turf for generations, the grizzly has a practical place in the environment. Such is the stuff of legend.

Fear is a strong motivator and many of the myths were woven with fear as their fabric. Knud Rasmussen, an Arctic explorer, asked a definition of belief from an eastern Arctic Eskimo and was told, "We do not believe, we only fear."

But the human mind is capable of so many more things than fear, namely respect and practicality. The Eskimo hunter's belief that if in a courageous hunt he was mauled by a grizzly, he need only split the carcass of the animal and crawl inside to be healed is a belief born, not out of fear, but out of a genuine regard for the animal's strength.

Sharing the countryside with such a powerful animal has traditionally been a matter of respect, honor and practical wisdom. These human traits showed up in a very common Arctic myth that forbade mentioning the bear by name. Instead, it was called only "the Great One." The grizzly, like the black bear, was said to have great hearing powers and any ill-spoken word towards the animal risked the wrath of its power.

Burning a piece of rag, said one Interior myth, would mean safety from bears. But there were more practical beliefs as well. One method, described by an Eskimo woman many years ago, is very close to what bear experts today suggest. She said "If you meet a brown bear in the woods, you must stand still, you must not be running, not even move, not even blink, and the bear will know that you are a brave one and will not bother you."

Staying away from bears was one thing; deliberately hunting them was another. But the same emotions of fear, awe and respect were part of the hunt. Some hunters wore a tooth or a claw from a previous kill as a sign of their own power. Though, like the black bear, most hunters saw the act of hunting as the bear giving itself to the hunter for meat and hide to be used by the hunter's family.

An unnatural arrogance brought about by the advent of firearms sometimes makes it difficult for those who have never hunted with only a spear to fathom the depths of the old beliefs. Yet they were so deep that in some places remnants of them linger even today.

In the Interior not so many years ago, an Eskimo trapper came across a brown bear snared in one of his traps. He had heard all the stories of honorable trappers taking their knives and battling the trapped animal hand-to-hand as it would have been in the old days. It was nonsense, he thought, and so he took out his small caliber trapping pistol and began firing. The shots only enraged the bear until it tore loose from the trap and mauled the man. A lucky shot finally killed the bear but not until the trapper was badly

Like a dance of autumn the salmon come upstream to spawn and the grizzlies gather at the river. This abundant food source is one of the main reasons for the differences in size between bears of the inland and bears of the coast (right).

injured, the weight of the dead bear pinning him to the ground.

After hours of struggle under the hot, bloody bear, the trapper managed to free himself and crawl back to his village where he told his story and begged for someone to bring him the bear's hide so that he might be wrapped in it and healed. After hearing the dishonorable way the man had acted, no one, not even his family, would bring him the hide. The man died of his wounds not long after.

Even though hand-to-hand combat was the most honorable method to battle the great bears, it was not the most practical in an environment where meat and hides could provide the staples through the long winter. To bring down the big, powerful animals some strange and unusual methods were tried.

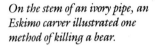

On the stem of an ivory pipe, an Eskimo carver illustrated one method of killing a bear.

One southwestern Alaska tribe cut planks and drove wooden spikes through them. The planks were then laid across a known bear trail and hidden with grass and baited. As a bear charged in for the bait, it would step directly on the spikes crippling itself. The hiding hunters would then rush it and make an end of the wounded animal with spears.

Eyak hunters of the southeastern part of the state had an even more risky method. The shafts of many sharp spears were driven into the ground with the tips angled forward and just far enough apart for an agile man to slip between them. One swift runner would then torment a nearby bear until it charged him. Racing for the spears with the bear inches behind, the hunter would nimbly dodge between the spears while the bear's momentum impaled it.

Despite the trickery sometimes used to bring it down, great respect was shown the dead animal and many of the same kinds of rituals observed for the black bear were followed by hunters of the grizzly.

Hunting meant meat, a good hide often used for the front door of winter huts to keep out the cold, quantities of fat used for many things, as well as claws and teeth for decoration. Use of the meat varied greatly among peoples. In the villages of northeastern Alaska, bear meat was thought too powerful to be eaten by any but the most skilled hunters. Some thought the meat poisonous and left it at the kill.

In some cases, poisonous meat may not have been far from the truth. Bears which survive mainly on a diet of roots and carrion, like those of the Interior, are often infected with a parasite known as *Trichanella* which causes trichinosis in humans when undercooked meat is eaten. Even today many Natives will not be persuaded to eat the meat of a grizzly. But in coastal areas where the bear survives on a diet of fish and berries, jars of bear fat can be found on the tables of many Native homes.

According to another myth, grizzlies had one more power that even other bear species did not possess—the ability to transfer its strength to humans. Few people in recent times have claimed such a tie with grizzlies. There is, however, the story of a man who died in Barrow around 1955. Villagers claimed the man had "particular affinities" with the grizzly. On the day of his funeral at the local Presbyterian church, a grizzly was seen wandering the streets, an uncommon sight that far north. The local people called it the rebirth of the man's spirit as a bear.

Fear. Respect. Awe. Arrogance. Legend often provides a clearer vision than reality itself. Like the Indian girl leaning over the still pond, we look into the deep waters of bear mythology and see, more than anything, ourselves.

P AST AND FUTURE. In 1691, an Englishman named Henry Kelsy was leading an expedition in the area of the Nelson River in northern Canada when the party surprised a grizzly on a moose kill. The bear treed the party to a man. While in the safety of the branches, Kelsy shot the animal and was dubbed "the Little Giant" by his men. The expedition continued.

It is thought that the grizzly shot by Kelsy was the first in the Northwest to feel the sting of gunpowder. The shot rang in a new era of man's relationship to wildlife, an era that would teach some bitter lessons.

Historically, the range of grizzlies took in a large part of the lower forty-eight states, as far east as Kansas and as far south as southern Texas. While few grizzlies today range anywhere but isolated patches of protected lands in the lower states, the reputation of Alaskan grizzlies was earned, at least in part, by the attitudes towards the bears that once roamed far and wide. To understand our view of Alaskan grizzlies, we must look briefly at the history of bears elsewhere.

While Kelsy was shooting bears from the treetops in the Northwest, Spanish conquistadores had a more gruesome entertainment devised for California grizzlies. Longhorn bulls were the measure of power in the Spaniard's world. Explorers brought back grizzlies in cages and pitted them against the bulls in large arenas. The bulls, powerful as they were, held no chance against a grizzly. With speed and power honed to a sharp edge by thousands of years in the wild, the grizzly would quickly crush the skull of the bull.

To even the odds, the bear would be chained by its hind legs, blinded by a slash across the eyes and then pummeled by bull after bull until it fell,

THE SUPERNATURAL GRIZZLY-BEAR-OF-THE-SEA
(Medeegem-dzawey[1]aks)

A pair of men were fishing on the sea in calm waters when an enormous grizzly sprang out of the water and smashed their boat to little bits, it is said in revenge for an act against the Mountain Goat people. Even from the waters, the fishermen, who were also great hunters, speared the bear and killed it. They could tell it was a sea-bear because of the human face on its fin and long human hair. Glad at their trophy, they tore out the hair, took the claws and cut off the beast's head.

Their knives were not yet done with the last cut when a strange and eerie foam began to rise out of the sea. It grew to cover the water. It grew to cover the trees. It grew to cover the mountain tops and scared the hunters.

First, they threw the hair back into the sea and the foam went down to the trees. Then they threw away the claws and the foam went down until it only covered the sea. Next, they composed a song and made a feast and the foam went away.

The hunters kept the head and showed it at all the feasts and whenever they sang the song. Today you will find the grizzly-bear-of-the-sea and its sea-brother the killer whale, on totem poles near the sea, together.

paraphrased from the
Totem Pole Indians
by Joseph Wherry

35

exhausted, with a score of slaughtered bulls around it.

Just as these sporting events delighted the Spaniards, tales of grizzlies aroused the interest of the reading public on America's eastern seaboard. One of the first glimpses of the grizzly of the West came with the publication of the Lewis and Clark Expedition of 1806. These journals remained the sole source of popular information on bears for many years to follow and so had a profound effect on the image of the "great white bare." The pages of the journals seemed charred with gunpowder as the men shot at nearly every bear they saw, in range or not.

In one memorable incident, Captain Lewis set off alone following a river in hopes of bringing back meat for the camp. Not far from camp he spotted a buffalo, bringing it down with a single shot. In the rush to get the meat back to camp, Lewis forgot to reload his gun immediately as was the habit of all good woodsmen of the time and began to butcher the animal. Hearing a stirring behind him, he turned to face a large grizzly attracted by the buffalo kill. The cool-headed Captain had already shot many bears on this expedition and had his mind on visions of bringing home bear meat on top of the buffalo. Reaching for his gun, he slowly lowered the barrel to draw a bead and pulled the trigger. A harmless "click" was all he heard.

The bear charged and the Captain ran weaving towards the river, where he dove in expecting the current to sweep him to safety. Unfortunately for the Captain, the water was only knee deep and the bear still charging. Scared, wet, tired and a long way from his home in the East, Lewis could think of no other defense than to face the bear with his dukes. He struck a classic boxing pose standing up to his knees in the river and waited.

The bear slid to a halt at the edge of the water, sitting back on its haunches to view this miserable sight, and then turned back for the now unguarded meat. Lewis, in the classic understated prose style of the time, proclaimed himself "very glad to be released from this danger." He returned to camp, presumably without any meat.

It is one thing to read about such epic encounters in the safety of the parlor but quite another to live them. As the settlers spread west in the wake of the Lewis and Clark Expedition, the stories became stark reality. Livestock replaced buffalo and gave grizzlies a slow-witted prey even easier to bring down than the longhorn bulls of the conquistadors. Tales of whole herds of cattle wiped out while terrified settlers huddled in their dim sod houses found their way back to government agencies, proof that, as one writer put it, "clearly, there is no place for it [the grizzly] in settled country." This "settled country" was expanding rapidly and what was once grizzly country was quickly becoming wheat fields and livestock range. The grizzly was being pushed out.

Although the guns and poisons of predator control programs took their toll, the real damage to the bear was done with the axe and the plow. The

In what sometimes seems like a barren landscape, grizzly cubs will stay with the sow for up to 4 years learning the ways of survival (left).

Tlingit war knife, ca. mid-1800s.

37

grizzly is a species which needs large expanses of uncivilized land to roam. Settled country does not allow that. As the habitat was cut down, fenced off and plowed under, the bears went, victims of the same strength and dominance that helped them survive for thousands of years. That, and their overwhelming affect on the human mind. The same traits which made the bear a legend, made it an outlaw.

So they went. Texas lost its last grizzly in 1890, shot as a stock killer. California's grizzly, which ironically remains its state emblem, went in 1922. Arizona records the date with the poignant accuracy of a tombstone— September 13, 1935. The Colorado Rockies went silent in 1952 except for a lone sow killed in the San Juan Mountains in 1979. Grizzlies have not been confirmed in the state since that day.

Alaska did not sit unnoticed during all this time. Already considered "the last frontier" by early in this century, it was facing many of the same pressures which destroyed the grizzly population elsewhere. Early game laws passed in 1908 were an attempt to ease those pressures before they could build but even these laws left room for a lot of local interpretation.

These laws stipulated that a "brown bear" may be shot anytime above the latitude of 62 degrees north. Below that point, which runs approximately sixty miles north of Anchorage, there would be a three-bear limit and a set season. In addition, only two permits a year were allowed each hunter for the exportation of the valuable hides. This, for all practical purposes, would have shut down the hunting since most of the pressure was felt in the more popu-lated areas below the dividing line where the regulations were the most strict. But in a state which has always seen itself as rugged and self-governing, laws were seen as an affront and trouble was brewing.

To make matters even more complicated, the confusion over the taxo-nomic differences between a grizzly and a brown bear was in its heyday. Playing on that confusion, Thomas Christmas Riggs, governor of the territory of Alaska, proclaimed that a "brown bear" was not a grizzly and so was not subject to the restrictive 1908 laws. In a speech, Riggs proclaimed that, "the brown bear has no place in the economic development of the Territory anymore than the herds of wild buffalo would have in the wheat fields of Minnesota or the Dakotas." His allusion to the buffalo left little doubt as to the plight Thomas Christmas Riggs wished on the bear population of Alaska.

But for the Presidential election of 1920 the rest of the story of grizzlies in Alaska might have read much differently. President-elect Harding quickly set about appointing a new, more forward-thinking governor to the territory and more comprehensive game laws were enacted.

The new game laws brought with them a new attitude and philosophy which has held in many ways up to the present. There are still, and in Alaska always will be, debates over land-use and game laws among the strongly independent population, both Native and non-Native. But most have come to see the place of bears in the state as a symbol and as an economic base for sport hunting and tourism. Today, Alaskans are proud of the grizzly population which is at, or above, historic levels. The unstable political situations which rock the management of grizzlies in places like Yellowstone National Park in Wyoming, as well as potential gas and oil conflicts in the Overthrust Belt which threatens the Montana grizzlies, could mean that in the not-too-distant future Alaska could become the last stronghold for this species.

Alaska is grizzly country. A great deal of the state's area is prime habitat and, ironically, lessons learned in places like Yellowstone National Park about the need to preserve entire ecosystems and habitats, have led to the designation of huge chunks of bear habitat as parks, wilderness areas, preserves and refuges. The Alaska National Interest Lands Settlement Act of 1980 was a conservation landmark for many reasons. None of the reasons is more important than the fact that the boundary work of the Act sought to delineate lands by ecosystems rather than by the straight-edge of survey teams. The 104 million acres of land set aside by the Act encompasses the most straightforward admission by the public that grizzlies are to be a part of Alaska and our future.

Grizzly habitat means salmon streams, berry patches and denning sites. It means meadows to forage and hillsides to dig for ground squirrels. And, it means space. Distance is inherent in the animal. Males can cover more than 1000 square miles in search of mates and food. Grizzlies need habitat with horizons. Habitat for some animals—deer, elk, moose—can be manipulated. For grizzlies, habitat can only be preserved.

Satellite photography, radio tracking and other research efforts will be needed to help insure that this habitat is identified. Then, the choices will have to be made. Discovery of huge oil and gas reserves on the North Slope beneath wildlife refuges, increased recreational use of newly-designated parks, development of road systems and pipelines will all make the picture of the bear's future even more complex.

The grizzly, even without all the outside factors, is a complex creature, unalterably entwined in its environment, a product of it and a part in it. The force that the animal can be on a landscape can be seen in the hollowness of the silent mountains and empty prairies of the lower forty-eight states. When the links are broken, the grizzlies are gone.

Attitude is more difficult to pinpoint than habitat types. There are no satellite photographs of public opinion. But Alaska has begun to designate places like the McNeil River State Game Sanctuary which was "established and is being managed to protect the concentration of bears," and where "all human use is of secondary importance to this objective."

An animal like the grizzly cannot survive only in sanctuaries anymore than it could in zoos, but it is a start. We are beginning, perhaps, to realize a simple but profound fact: Man is a visitor in grizzly country. Almost by definition grizzly country is a place where human presence is not dominant, an environment shaped by other forces. One of these forces is the grizzly. The sight of tracks brings the country alive with possibilities.

It is the possibility of coming over a rise to find a sow and her twin cubs trotting out the next ridgeline or of rounding a bend in the trail to come face to face with a surly male. It is a sense of privilege in walking the same creekbed as the bear, sharing the same horizons. You carry it with you like your pack and in sleep it wraps around you like a blanket. All such places have it—cathedrals, summits, deep canyons—this sense of privilege. So it is with grizzly country.

And so it must be if the grizzly is to remain on the landscape. That is its place, not as some "demigod of the past" roaming the mythologies, but in the high meadows and down along some Arctic river where it can follow the bend upstream or turn and strike for the mountains.

With the first snows of winter already dusting the high peaks, the grizzly feels the first stirrings of the long sleep, searching the river bottoms for salmon to add layers of fat against the deep winter to come.

THE BROWN/ GRIZZLY BEAR

Ursus arctos horribilis

by Harry V. Reynolds
Alaska Department of Fish and Game

DISTRIBUTION & CLASSIFICATION

Grizzly bears live throughout most of Alaska except the islands of the Aleutian Chain west of Unimak Island and the islands south of Frederick Sound.

When describing these bears both brown and grizzly is correct; however, "brown bear" usually refers to those found in southern and coastal areas, while "grizzly bear" refers to inland and northern bears. Technically, all brown or grizzly bears (except those on Kodiak Island) belong to the same species and subspecies. Bears living on Kodiak Island have been given the separate subspecific name *Ursus arctos middendorffi*. However, there appears to be little difference between the size, population biology or behavior of bears on Kodiak Island and the nearby mainland bear population.

PHYSICAL CHARACTERISTICS

The predominant shoulder hump and long claws, two of the physical characteristics which set the grizzly apart from black bears or polar bears, are closely tied to food gathering habits. Both have evolved for digging roots and rodents.

Color variations appear to be related to habitat use. Although all colors from blonde to dark brown may be found in most populations, lighter colors appear to be more prevalent in open habitats such as the tundra portions of Arctic and Interior Alaska. In areas where bears use darker, more forested habitats, grizzled, brown and dark brown appear with more frequency.

Size and weight vary according to availability of food. On the Arctic Slope, the growing season is short and few berries or salmon are available. The mainstay of the diet in this region consists of roots, vegetation, ground squirrels and an occasional caribou calf or adult. In this area, adult males average 380 to 450 pounds and can reach up to 600 pounds or more. Adult females average 200 to 240 pounds, but rarely exceed 400 hundred pounds.

In contrast, in coastal Alaska where summers are mild, vegetation lush and salmon runs plentiful, males range from 600 to 1000 pounds and can reach 1400 hundred pounds and more. Females in this area range from 400 hundred to 700 pounds.

HABITAT USE & HOME RANGE

An adaptive nature has given these bears the ability to exploit a wide range of habitat types. Quality of habitat determines many aspects of the bear's natural history. Habitat quality includes availability of vegetation, length of growing season, weather extremes and availability of additional food sources such as spawning salmon, ground squirrels and moose calves. Availability and nutrient content of foods used by bears varies greatly in Alaska's diverse habitat types. These variations in habitat quality result in the differences of physical characteristics and reproductive biology across the state.

Grizzlies do not occupy and defend fixed territories but they do live in fairly well-defined areas called "home ranges." The home range of one bear may overlap broadly with those of many other grizzlies. Size of these home ranges are probably dependent upon the availability of food resources. Where these resources are plentiful (such as on Kodiak Island) average home range for a female is only six square miles. On the Arctic Slope where resources are more scarce, average home range for a female is one hundred and thirty-three square miles.

Males, which travel more widely for food, mates and denning sites, have average home ranges two to four times larger than that of females. The largest home range, one thousand eight hundred square miles, was recorded in northwestern Alaska.

Within their home ranges males may move an average of three and eight-tenths miles per day and females two and a half miles per day.

BEHAVIOR

Grizzly bears have a solitary nature. Other than groups which consist of a mother and offspring, grizzlies rarely have social contact. Exceptions occur during the breeding season or at especially abundant food sources. During times of congregation an established dominance heirarchy or pecking order exists to

Size—Length 6–8 feet
Height 3–4 feet
Weight 400–1200 lbs. (m)
200–700 lbs. (f)
Diet—Omnivorous
Habitat—Forest/Tundra
Color—Blonde/Dark Brown

minimize aggressive interactions.

Regardless of her place in the pecking order, a mother grizzly will defend her offspring against any perceived threat, including a larger, more dominant bear. Defense is not always successful against larger bears and there is evidence that adult males may seek out and kill offspring, especially newborn cubs.

POPULATION BIOLOGY Grizzly bears breed during late May to early July. An individual female is receptive for ten to fourteen days. A pair may stay together during the entire receptive cycle. Often, however, a female may have more than a single mate.

After the female is impregnated, the embryo grows only a short time and then stays dormant until denning in October, allowing the buildup of fat reserves for the winter. If fat deposition is not sufficient for the nurturing of cubs, the embryo probably aborts.

From one to four cubs are born by early February. The average litter size varies due to the availability of food resources. The young weigh only about one pound but will gain up to fifteen pounds by the time they emerge from the den in May and will weigh over seventy pounds when they enter the dens again in late fall. Grizzly cubs den with their mother for several winters.

The age at which females begin to produce young and the intervals between litters varies substantially across the state. In extreme northern Alaska, females may not produce a first litter until ten years of age. On the Alaska Peninsula, one of the most productive populations in the state, young are produced by the fifth or sixth year. Females may continue to produce young up to their twenty-seventh year, the maximum normal lifespan.

Weaning times also vary. In areas such as northern Alaska, grizzlies usually keep their young until the fourth summer. On the Alaska Peninsula, offspring are weaned in the spring of their third year. Such variations in reproductive biology are responsible for the differences in population densities throughout the state.

DENNING Grizzlies may spend more of their lives in the den than being active. Denning can start as early as late September and last until mid-May, but the length of this dormant period depends on sex, age, reproductive status and weather conditions. Females that give birth to cubs during the denning period tend to stay in the den the longest; mature males, the shortest. New dens are usually dug each year and may be far removed from previous dens. Natural caves are sometimes used year after year.

Outside temperatures may reach minus sixty degrees. To conserve body heat bears require the insulation of fur, body fat and den construction. Den construction begins after the first layer of soil freezes providing the necessary structural support for the den. A typical den is dug on a steep hillside or dirt bank and has an upward-leaning tunnel ending in a large chamber lined with grasses or vegetation. With the coming snows, the entrance is drifted over and closed.

THE FUTURE At present, grizzly bear populations in Alaska are flourishing. Except in populated areas, there are probably as many or more grizzlies than there have been within the last fifty years. Sport hunting occurs throughout the state with the exception of national parks and state sanctuaries, but is closely monitored and controlled. Grizzly populations are managed as an important natural resource by professional biologists. Research is being conducted to supplement our present knowledge of grizzly biology and improve management strategies in every region of Alaska.

Many aspects of grizzly bear biology which have contributed to their former wide distribution and success as a species have created conflicts with humans. The grizzly is curious, highly adaptable, has omnivorous food habits and has much variation in individual behavior. These characteristics have brought the species into direct competition with humans.

The future of the grizzly in Alaska depends on preservation of bear habitat. In order to assure that the grizzly continues to roam this wild country, land managing agencies may have to restrict logging, agriculture and resource development activities in areas where the potential for conflict is apparent.

POLAR BEAR
ICE & SEA & SKY

ICE. Miles of white ice broken only by the jagged lines of pressure ridges where the sea below has grown restless. Sky, in all directions it seems to roll off the horizons. Cold that can freeze a man's spit before it hits the ice. This is winter off the northern coast of Alaska—dark, cold, barren. Barren, but not lifeless.

Of all the creatures on the ice—the fox, the raven, the seal and walrus—it is the polar bear which is the symbol of this place. Its coat, its form like wind-blown ice, its motion, all seem to make it a natural outcropping of such an environment.

The world roamed by polar bears seems myth-like to most. Any creature which inhabits such an environment must itself be something of a myth. That is the polar bear.

If the grizzly is the symbol of a vanished or vanishing West, the polar bear is the symbol of the eternal North. It is a landscape and an animal which exist only in legend for many people, a place frozen in time, an animal which gets its breath from the howling winds, its coat from the clouds, and what flows in its veins from the icy seas.

To the few who know this part of the world and its bear, it is a place of stark realities and an animal which has come to grips with its environment in some very realistic ways.

ARCTIC REALITIES. The first reality hits like the steel blade of a spear: cold. Temperatures in winter can reach minus 70 degrees with winds that can rip flesh from the bone. In cold like this the body's inner core hoards the heat for the vital organs, shutting down the blood flow to the extremities. The extremities of the polar bear are equipped for such a hoarding with hollow bones filled with an oily marrow that keeps what heat there is more efficiently. Thick blubber layers provide insulation over the rest of the body. Over the blubber is a thick, oily and dark-colored skin. Over that, a heavy coat of waterproof fur.

THE POLAR BEAR & THE HUNTER

In Point Hope there lived a polar bear hunter. Everytime he went hunting, this man caught and killed a polar bear. Once, on a hunt, he saw a polar bear and ran far ahead of the other hunters until he was so far out on the ice he couldn't see the mountains any more or any of the other hunters. Then, the polar bear stopped running and turned to face the hunter as he drew back his spear. The bear charged but the hunter dodged aside. The hunter jabbed at the bear with his spear but the spear did not hit the bear. They kept sparring with each other until they were both very tired. Finally, the bear stood up in front of the hunter and took the cover off his head. It was a young boy, hot and sweating and wearing all kinds of beads around his neck. The polar bear said "You are hard to get. All these years I have killed men, taking their beads and putting them on this string around my neck until my string is full. This is the first time I did not kill a man." The hunter answered, "All these years I've been killing polar bear and this is the first time I didn't kill one."

As they talked, it grew dark and cold and the hunter was still far from home. The polar bear told him, "Stay here for the night. You won't be cold." The man went to sleep on the polar bear's stomach and all night he wasn't cold.

paraphrased from
The Eskimo Storyteller: Folktales from Noatak, Alaska
by Edwin S. Hall, Jr.

Despite all of this, the bear's real secret to survival in this frozen place may lie in something as light as the sun's rays. Hold a strand of polar bear fur to the light and it is not white at all but translucent and hollow. Some researchers believe that sunlight, heat in the form of ultraviolet light, is conducted from the tips of the outer coat through the hollow hairs and into the heat-absorbing skin. In this way the animal synonymous with ice and snow may actually be solar heated.

The second reality of the polar bear's world is hunger. The sea ice is a frozen desert with no vegetation and a low density of animal life. The polar bear lives in nearly constant search of food. Of all the North American bear species only the polar bear can be considered a true predator. Its main prey is the ringed seal.

To understand the predator, you must understand the prey. Seals are mammals built for the sea, awkward on land but dance-like in the water. As a mammal it must return to the surface for air at regular intervals. It is the moment at the surface that polar bears thrive on.

When the ice is forming on the last open water in early winter seals become limited to an area only as large as the number of breathing holes or *aglus* that can be kept open by the persistent clawing of flippers. A snow-covered aglu is nearly impossible to detect with the naked eye. How the bear so expertly picks out the spots on the ice is not fully understood, but there are theories.

Seals, particularly the *tiggak* or rutting males, give off a strong odor which must be detectable to the nose of a polar bear which is said to be capable of scenting a rotting whale on a beach twenty miles across open water.

There could be other ways. When surfacing to breathe seals sometimes let out a sharp hissing noise that can be heard a good distance in the Arctic stillness. Or, it could be keen eyesight. Bears are very curious about even the slightest irregularity in the ice and have been known to come for miles to investigate holes drilled in the ice by research crews collecting water.

Or, and most likely, it is a combination of all of these and more. In an environment as complex as that of the sea ice no possibility can be overlooked.

A stalking bear never meets the same conditions twice and so must be flexible in its hunting techniques. The challenge has honed the polar bear into the consummate seal hunter. If the ice is thin near an *aglu,* it may rear up and smash the ice around the seal as it rises. If it is too thick, the bear may scrape away a layer of ice around the hole and wait.

This long, patient wait at a hole in the sea ice has been the subject of many legends. The most often heard is the claim that the bear hides its nose with its paw as it waits. Topsell, a seventeenth-century zoologist, claimed it was to disguise its breath which he described this way "Bears do send forth such a breath that it putrifies immediately the flesh of dogs or what-so-ever beast comes within savor thereof."

Others, like Arctic explorer Vihjalmur Stefansson, claim it is because the dark spot of its nose gives its position away. "No stone, no bare spot in the snow, no dark shadow is as black as the polar bear's nose," Stefansson says, "It is unmistakable miles away."

The black spot of the great white bear's nose has been the focus of nearly as many tales as the fangs of the grizzly. It is told that the bear sometimes pushes chunks of ice ahead of it as it stalks, extends its tongue to cover it as it hunts, and even packs snow around it to conceal the blackness. Scientific studies have just begun on the habits of the polar bear and although Canadian researchers have logged over 5,000 hours of field observation the polar bear still spends most of its life beyond the scrutiny of man's vision. For now, myths like those surrounding the polar bear's black nose remain just a part of the mystery and lure of this legendary creature.

With its nose in the snow or not, the wait at an *aglu* can be a long one. Bears have been observed sitting motionless at an *aglu* for 72 hours without making a kill. Hunched there on the ice, still but for the wind in its fur, the polar bear takes on the look of its world. It becomes pack ice with heart. At certain angles each of the colors and textures of sea ice can be seen in its fur. The polar ice sheet is not a featureless plain but a menagerie of shapes and forms changing with the wind and the tides. Too, the coat of a polar bear is not a monotonous coat of white, it is a tangle of wind and animal, a reflection of the world around it as the bear waits there on the ice.

The utter stillness of the scene is shattered dramatically at the moment of attack. For all its wariness, the seal has one fatal flaw. As it rises to the surface to exhale, for that one instant, it can neither hear nor detect scent. It is enough for the polar bear to make its move.

The end is sudden. A stirring below the ice and with a single motion the bear has crushed the ice and sunk its teeth deep into the seal, ripping it from the sea with such force that the animal is crushed and dead before the air is out of its lungs.

Waiting on the ice, or "still hunting," is only one of the ways polar bears take seals. They will also stalk seals sunning out on the ice in a sort of Arctic "blind Man's bluff," or take them out of open water. A bear will take any opportunity. It must.

It is thought that an adult bear needs to take as many as fifty ringed seals a year, an average of nearly one a week, to maintain its prime condition. For every seal taken there may be several that slip back to the safety of the sea.

Illingworth, in his book entitled *Wildlife Beyond the North*, tells of watching a bear stalking a seal across the ice for over an hour, stopping when the seal looked back, edging closer as the seal lowered its head, only to miss at the last moment as the seal slipped back into the water. The bear, Illingworth reports, went into a rage, slamming its paws into the ice so savagely that it

A small part of the bear's power was left, like warmth, in its fresh tracks. Coming across the fresh prints of a bear among the hummocks, a circle was cut around the freshest track and it was lifted from the ice. Each hunter ate a small piece, taking in the power, before moving on into the jumbled ice to begin the hunt.

"broke every bone in its right hand and severely injured its left." Still, success in such an environment is survival and the polar bear has won enough times in the workings of seal and bear to have become a survivor.

BATTLES ON THE ICE. Historically the polar bear has had few enemies on the ice. Its size and strength are nearly unmatched—nearly.

Weighing up to a ton and a half with three-foot tusks of piercing ivory, the bull walrus can be the formidable exception to the polar bear's rein as king of the ice. It is rare for a polar bear to attack a mature walrus but there are stories that are told.

Peter Fruechen, an Arctic explorer, came across an eerie and silent death scene which told the tale of a great unwitnessed battle:

> It is generally accepted that no animal can overcome a walrus. Occasionally, we have seen a dead bear found close to the edge of the ice or on a hummock with gaping puncture wounds. Probably he tried to snatch a pup away from a mother walrus and the fight that resulted ended with the long and powerful tusks piercing the bear's ribs.

Illingworth came closer to seeing the battle with his own eyes when he watched from his ship as a polar bear stalked three bull walrus sunning on a shelf. As the bear tensed for its final lunge, the largest of the bulls turned and:

> Exactly what happened next, I cannot say. But, in a matter of seconds the bear lay bleeding from a mortal wound and the old bull, roaring angrily, lifted itself on its flippers and surveyed the scene of victory before taking to the water.

Lamont, in an 1876 publication *Yachting the Arctic Seas*, saw the poignant results of a battle floating in the icy grave of the sea. From the rail of his ship he spotted the frozen carcasses of a polar bear and a walrus floating just below the water locked in a death grip. As if it had reared up atop the walrus the bear's claws were dug deep into the opponents skull, while the tusks of the walrus were driven nearly through the chest of the polar bear. There they floated for a moment as the crew looked on, then sank beneath the dark water.

The same narrative tells another gruesome tale. Seeing a large polar bear swimming far from shore, the crew gathered to watch and saw a herd of walrus appear from beneath the bear and pull it down out of sight in the water. As the boat sailed on with the crew watching the spot where the bear disappeared, only chunks of floating hair and flesh appeared at the surface.

There are more stories, tales of polar bears lifting chunks of ice over their

Ancient myths link the polar bear with the killer whale and with its habitat of sea ice the polar bear is as much a creature of the water as of the land (left).

Head of a swimming bear. Soapstone sculpture, ca. 1969.

heads to smash the skull of a young walrus or swimming underneath a small iceberg to tip a small seal from the safety of its perch. Relative to other North American mammals very little has been documented in the area of polar bear behavior. With its remote and harsh habitat, even today, many bears live and die without ever seeing a human form on the ice. It is an animal hidden by time, climate and distance. Even as more tales are researched and verified or refuted, there will remain more that is left unknown than is known about the life of the polar bear.

RELEASING THE FORM: CARVING IN IVORY. The carvings of the northern Eskimos resemble nothing so much as ice which has taken on an artful form. No other art form seems to spring so directly from the environment. Carved in the ivory of walrus tusks, the color is that of the smoky mists that rise over freezing waters. Even in the brightly-lit gift shops of Anchorage and Fairbanks, the chill of the ice comes through when a piece of ivory sculpture is held in your hand, particularly a carving of a polar bear.

Carving in ivory, the old way, is a sometimes practice in strict reality. The work of certain artists is often so accurate that the species can be told at a glance. Detail is a matter of pride. Such precision is the reflection of a practical and observant mind and the realities of Eskimo culture. Artists, before the commercialization of their work, were also hunters. In their carvings were the cold winds and frozen days of the hunts, the stalk across the ice, the flight of the spears through the cold air. Carvings were done from the memory of the bear in the instant before the spears struck.

There is another side to Eskimo carving in ivory, much the same as the carving of wooden bear masks or totem poles. It was believed that all creation, including the piece of ivory, had a spirit. The carver would toss the piece of ivory in his hand for hours hoping that it would reveal to him its inner form. He thought himself less an artist than one who released that form.

With the spirits not chained to a single, unchanging form, the carvings often took varied shapes. As an expression of the bond between man and animal, some pieces showed the forms of man evolving from the bear. As the authors of *The Far North* put it, "In Eskimo thought where spirit is regarded as separate from flesh and each man has many helping spirits, the line between species and class, even between man and animal, are lines of fusion not fission and nothing has a single, invariable shape." Depiction of these "lines of fusion" has led to some of the most beautiful works of art from the Eskimo culture.

Unlike mask-carving and totem poles which were more deeply entwined with religious practices that have fallen from use, carving was more for pleasure and is still practiced today. And it was found to be profitable as well. Carvers discovered early the potential of tourism dollars in their work. This profit motivation has led to some dilution of the form. Salt and pepper shakers, an item which had no place in historic Eskimo life, became a popular item for carvers since the tourist thought them cute. The "six-legged bear" which shows two bears copulating became a kind of Native joke on the naive tourists and also became a popular subject for carvers.

The commercialization perhaps took something out of the artwork, still if you search the gift shops and the pawn brokers of the cities or visit the homes of carvers in the remote villages, you can yet find an occasional piece that seems as though it was carved from the icy heart of a bear. Holding it in your hand you feel the cold wind far out on the sea ice. You feel its hidden form released. Such pieces are rare, but then rarity is one of the dimensions in all great art.

A twentiety-century ivory carving gives form to the belief in bear-man transformation.

NEW FORM ON THE ICE: MAN. From the standpoint of evolution the polar bear is a fairly recent addition to the Arctic environment. Nevertheless, the bear which first looked across the ice at the silhouetted form of a human was little different than the bear of today. Man is the newcomer and since that first unrecorded meeting Man and bear have shared the icescape for over 10,000 years. Until very late in this history the effects have shown more on humans than on the bear.

Out hunting on the ice, an Eskimo spots a pair of ravens flying overhead and calls up *nanu-quapi?*, or "are there bear?" The hunter is wearing polar bear skins on his feet to silence his approach. Wearing white like the bear, the hunter will later hunch over an *aglu* and, again like the bear, sit motionless to wait.

The best hunters took notice of the bear and often made close use of the techniques learned by its hunting, not only when hunting seals but also when hunting the bear itself. The hunter would move only when the wind rustled, hide behind ice chunks, freeze when the bear turned its head.

Then, too, the good hunters knew of and used to their advantage the great curiosity of polar bears. If out hunting alone the man would lie on the ice and "play seal" by slowly raising and lowering his upper body off the ice. The motions attracted the curious bear and lured it close enough for the spear. Even today in villages along the coast it is not uncommon to see children out on the ice "playing seal."

Or, if the hunters were in a group, one man would be sent out on the ice alone to begin a crazed and furious dance. The motions of a man jumping and twirling can be seen for miles on the flat ice and any bear in the area would come closer to investigate.

It was said that polar bear hunts were special. It was said that the hunters

needed the bear "not as a predator needs his prey, but as a challenge to reaffirm his own ability." There may be some truth in such a view but it is best also to remember the hardships and challenges of mere survival in such an environment. Surely there was honor in bringing down such a powerful creature, but there was also meat, hide, fat and bones.

With the size of a polar bear, the meat and other parts were often shared throughout the village. It was traditional for a call to go out through the village that a polar bear had been taken and for the villagers to gather for the butchering. Choice parts, such as the hindquarters, were the property of the hunter who made the kill. The rest was divided among the villagers.

The pelt of the polar bear was, and still is, very valuable. It was sometimes made into pants for the hunter and a good-sized hide would be enough for three pairs of the highly-prized pants. As the demand for bear rugs and trophies increased from areas outside the villages fewer of the hunters kept the hides. A single pelt could bring between $100 and $1,000 depending on its size and quality. Polar bear pants today are rare.

While many of the rituals of the North have been lost, remnants can still be seen at times. The Eskimo hunter who took the first polar bear of the season a few years ago at Barrow did not make polar bear pants as before but he did go around offering others a share of the meat until he had only a small portion for himself. The part he kept—the hindquarters.

Taste for polar bear meat, like the meat of all bears, varies. While most Natives prize it, many non-Native palates find it oily and fat. Frozen, its texture is best described as ice cream. Cooked, the most graphic description comes from Lael Morgan who says:

> It did not appeal to me. It was rather like last Thursday's pot roast basted with cod-liver oil. But, I swallowed three pieces and came to appreciate it. With a little polar bear meat under your belt you can walk for five hours and never feel cold. Of course you belch all day no matter what you eat afterwards, but it is a small price to pay to keep from freezing to death.

One part of the bear that was usually avoided was the liver. It is so saturated with vitamin A that it is nearly poisonous. "Only the raven can eat it," says one Eskimo story. Most hunters will not bring it back from the kill or will only feed it to their dogs. A Barrow man, alive today, tells of a hunt he recalls as a young boy. The party killed a polar bear and some of the hunters ate pieces of the liver and died. The man himself, just licking the blood off the knife used to cut the liver, fell ill. Though he survived, he lost the natural pigment of his hair and skin.

The journals of many early Arctic expeditions tell of whole parties being taken ill from eating the liver of bears, suffering severe headaches and loss of hair and skin.

THE FIRST BEARS

"Long ago on the shores of the Arctic Ocean, an Eskimo woman lived with her tribe. She already had several children but one day two children were born together. They were very strange twins indeed. One was covered with long white fur while the other had a coat of brown fur. Since they were not like any of her children, the mother did not want them. So one day she took them far from the igloo and left them alone. When she had gone, the white-furred child got up and ran down the beach and out across the frozen sea. The brown child turned his back to the sea and scrambled across the tundra and into the mountains. And there they have lived every since. But, people do not call them men. They are known as "Nanook" or Polar bear and Brown bear . . ."

Edward Keithah
Alaskan Igloo Tales

Eskimo carvings commonly depict a hole in the hand of the hunter to show that not all hunts were successful. Modern hunting techniques have closed that hole and in light of the slow reproductive rate of polar bears, strict hunting regulations are necessary to protect females and cubs (left).

53

"Somewhere far away, a man decided to go out on the ice to wait for an animal. He set out for the breather hole of a ten-legged polar bear. He knew a safe place to hide in case the bear attacked.

His hiding place was a large iceberg with a hole in through it—large on one side and small at the other.

People in those days knew the breather hole of the ten-legged polar bear had lungs floating on it.

When the ten-legged polar bear appeared at its breather hole,

the hunter poked out its eyes. When the polar bear began to climb out of the hole, the hunter fled. Staggering his steps to slow the bear, he headed for the iceberg.

When he finally got there, he headed for the hole and went right through it. The bear followed him but halfway through he got wedged in and could not get

These early explorers had encounters with more than just the livers of polar bears. The new forms on the ice attracted the naturally curious bears and the journals are filled with encounters. Some of them were humorous. The bear was known as "the farmer" for its country-like, bull-legged swagger. Humor, however, gave way to terror as the bears were seen for hours cutting the trails of the dogsled teams just at the edge of sight.

One camp of restless men near the northern coast took to feeding a bear. The sight of it wrestling with the new and strange packages helped to pass the long hours—until, one night after dinner, the cook was tossing scraps to the bear and slipped on the ice. The sudden motion frightened the bear and that was the end of the cook.

For all the adventure dreamed about in exploring the Arctic, often the sailors on exploratory vessels would get bored and begin taking pot-shots at anything on the ice. Members of the Brown Expedition of 1868 came upon "30 of the beasts" feeding on a whale carcass. As reported in the proceedings of the Zoological Society of London, some of the men were,

> . . . foolish enough to fire a few shots among them when the bears sprang furiously from the carcass and made for our boat. One succeeded in getting a paw across the gunwale and it was only by the vigorous application of an axe that we succeeded in relieving ourselves of so unwelcomed an addition to our crew.

These journals, like the journals of Lewis and Clark concerning the grizzly, became the only source of popular literature about this cold, mysterious land and its bear of ice. It was in these journals that many of the myths and legends were born.

One such legend involves the bear using chunks of ice as a weapon. In a story that rings the Arctic, reported in many early journals, it is said that "in combats between bears and walrus, the former frequently obtains victory by taking masses of ice and dashing them against the heads of their opponents." Ivory carvings from many parts of the Arctic display bears holding aloft chunks of ice. Although never verified by scientific observation in the wild, through the hole nor could be back out. The hunter, who had already gone all the way through came back around to the front and stabbed the bear in the back repeatedly and killed him.

He got some men to help him take the bear back to the village. It is said that the head was so big that the children used to play on it, climbing and sliding.

Itchaagak's wife remembered sliding on it when it was brought ashore when she was a little girl. Nasualuk and Aalguq also remember it.

It has not, however, been seen for a long time; probably buried in the sand or mud."

as told by Flyod Ahvakana,
Barrow, Alaska
translated by Leona Okakok

two polar bears at the London Zoo were seen to toss huge chunks of ice about the exhibit during the summer of 1962.

The strength of the animal has never been in question. Standing up to 12 feet tall and weighing over 1400 pounds, it rivals the brown bear for the distinction of being the largest carnivore to walk the earth today. Although its streamline profile and long neck make it seem less muscular than the compact shape of the grizzly, an adult male has little trouble ripping a 250-pound ring seal through a small hole in thick ice with a single twist of its strong neck and shoulders. Eskimos of northwest Alaska tell of seeing a bear easily tear into the frozen carcass of a walrus that even their metal axes could not cut.

A strange but often repeated tale says that the polar bear is left-handed. Eskimo stories tell of it ripping into prey with its left paw. Early journal reports of attacks say that the first charge was led with the left paw. Hunting stories during the days of the spear tell of hunters dodging to his left to escape the left-handed swipe of the on-coming bear. This is one tale which has been, at least partly, verified by science. Fred Bruemmer, in his *Encounters with Arctic Animals*, tells of a scientific snaring procedure in which twenty-one bears were captured. In the case of all twenty-one, the bear was snared by its left foreleg.

The tales have painted the polar bear as a killer. It is. The polar bear has reigned over its icy kingdom for more than 100,000 years. That existence is based almost solely on its ability to locate and bring down prey. It is the task for which evolution has sharpened its claws and teeth, camouflaged its coat and developed its keen hunting skills. Its role is domination of its world, a role it has played out to its fullest, at least until the coming of modern man to the Arctic.

It is cold, dark much of the year, nearly barren of life. Man, with his furless body and soft skin seems out of place in such an environment. It is a humbling experience to stand on the sea ice and look out to where the horizons blend in with the winter sky. But modern man did not come to the Arctic humbly.

We came with a racket, the racket of the ski plane. Hidden against the huge expanses of the sea ice, the polar bear was in little danger from hunters who came by land, on dogsleds or even the more modern snowmachines. The land was too big for that. But the advent of hunting trips by airplane changed the rules of the game and the bear began to lose. Hunters from all over the world would be flown by charter services out across the ice until a bear was spotted. Working in tandem, one plane would drop the hunter off as close as possible to the bear while the second herded the animal within range of the high-powered rifle.

With the rifle, the bear could be killed before it knew that humans were on the ground. When the crack of the rifle replaced the silent flight of the spear, the spatial and philosophical arrangement between the hunter and the hunted changed. Where once the bear was stalked until it met the eyes of the hunter before the spear was thrown, the rifle could drop a bear before it detected a shadow, a movement or caught a scent. The eyes of the living bear never met those of the hunter.

The numbers of bears taken each year rose dramatically. Record keeping was difficult but it is estimated that harvest levels averaged 117 animals in the years between 1925 and 1953. An increase in the price for its coat as well as access by ski planes pushed the number as high as 300 a year by 1965. In light of the scant data base gathered by scientists on the bears' population and reproduction rates, the harvest was continuing blindly. In a circumstance where it was much easier to kill a polar bear than to gather meaningful scientific data, knowledge was being outpaced by the killing.

An important meeting took place in Fairbanks, Alaska in 1965 with representatives from all the countries with an interest in polar bear management. At that meeting five countries reached an unprecedented agreement which set protection for female polar bears and their cubs as well as began a program of international cooperative research. With the passage of the Marine Mammal Protection Act of 1972, polar bear hunting in the United States was ended, except for Native subsistence hunting.

There are still problems; while the 1972 Act did put an end to aerial sport hunting, it still left pregnant females and cubs susceptible to Natives exercising their subsistence rights, but the research agreements are shedding new light on the polar bear and its world. The polar bear, finally, is entering the realm of scientific knowledge.

The seemingly untouchable habitat of the bear has also changed. Discovery of vast petroleum reserves, hydrocarbon development, even the dramatic increase in recreational and tourist use of the high Arctic have put the footsteps of humans where no footsteps have been seen before. As rugged and harsh as the habitat of the polar bear seems, its low productivity and fragile balance make it susceptible to rapid change. The best estimates now place the world's population of polar bears at between 20,000 and

40,000 animals. New regulations, designation of coastal areas as parks and refuges and management treaties are helping to keep the winds of change from blowing too hard on the polar bears and their habitat. It is a strange land, distant and hard to touch but if the polar bear is to survive the land and its bear can no longer remain a mystery and myth.

There will always be an element of mystique about the polar bear and the land it roams. It is a symbol of that place, of the tenacity and incredible diversity of life on earth. If the hunter once needed to kill the polar bear to "reaffirm his own ability," perhaps modern man needs to insure the bear's survival to reaffirm his own ability to understand and respect the purpose of life beyond the sound of his own heartbeat. If the polar bear should go, a part of our possible wisdom will go with it. There is an unknowable value in insuring the answer to the question called up to the ravens by the Eskimo hunter, *Nanu-qupai?*, "are there bears?"

Yes.

THE POLAR BEAR

Ursus maritimus

by Steven C. Amstrup
U.S. Fish and Wildlife Service

Size—Length 6–10 feet
Height 3–4 feet
Weight 600–1200 lbs.
Diet—Carnivorous
Habitat—Sea ice/Coast
Color—White/Creamy-off white

HISTORY AND DISTRIBUTION About one hundred thousand years ago when the great ice sheets advanced upon and dissected what is now known as Siberia, some ancestors of our modern-day grizzly bears forsook the land and took to the sea ice. Whether this move was by choice or otherwise, those bears experienced strong evolutionary pressures and dramatic changes occurred. Long straight claws—previously used for digging—became short, sharp and strongly curved for clinging to ice and seizing prey animals. Flat cheek teeth—once used for grinding plant matter—became sharper for shearing meat, blubber and hide. Fur density increased and hairs became hollow to ward off cold and, most noticeably, assumed a creamy white color to provide better camouflage in the white ice environment.

Today, polar bears occupy the entire sea ice-covered region of the Northern Hemisphere including lands and seas controlled by five nations: Denmark, Norway, Canada, the Soviet Union and the United States. In the United States, polar bears occur only in Alaska.

Sea ice dominates the coastal environments of northern and northwestern Alaska between late September and June. It is mainly then that the polar bears can be seen on or near the shore. When the sea ice expands to its maximum in late winter, polar bears can be found as far south as the Bering Strait and St. Lawrence Island. In summer, the ice retreats northward. When it does, most of Alaska's polar bears go with it, occupying the edge of the polar icecap where much of the sea remains ice-covered year-round.

Polar bears are quintessential wanderers, and scientists once thought individual bears traveled indiscriminately around the globe. We now know that most polar bears do not wander aimlessly, but occupy limited areas within which they move about according to the rhythm of the seasons. These areas are still large, however. Recent research has shown that many Alaskan polar bears travel over sea ice areas exceeding 100,000 square miles—an area almost as large as the state of Montana. Some wanderings may result from movements of the sea ice which, unlike land, is a dynamic platform upon which to live. But bears also move independently of the ice, and periods of unusual cold, sea currents, or wind can dramatically alter their distribution.

HABITS Polar bears will feed upon beached whales and other carrion when available. They have also been known to take young walruses. In Alaska, however, two species of seal—ringed and bearded—are the polar bear's mainstay. Seals are large and not easy prey to catch. A polar bear may catch two or three seals in a day and then catch none for several weeks. Thus, polar bears are well adapted to a feast or famine diet. They can store considerable energy as fat which also acts as insulation against the Arctic cold, and they can consume large quantities of food rapidly to take advantage of a short-term abundance. Polar bears are able to consume over ten percent of their body weight within thirty minutes, and the stomach of a large bear can hold up to 140 pounds of food at one time.

The absence of winter denning is one of the most obvious features distinguishing polar bears from the other North American bear species. While brown and black bears become dormant each winter, most polar bears remain active, foraging on the sea ice throughout the year. Although any polar bear may construct a temporary den to escape the cold or be sheltered against a severe storm, only pregnant females regularly den for extended periods. Dens typically consist of tunnels dug into snowbanks and enlarged by the mother and cubs as the winter progresses. Because dens are constructed only of snow, topographical features such as bluffs, ridges or hills behind which large snow drifts can accumulate are essential for denning. Most denning is thought to occur on land, and large concentration areas have been found in some other regions of the world. However, recent research has shown that the majority of maternity denning in Alaska is offshore in the drifting pack ice.

Cubs are typically born in December or January. Litters of two occur most often. Single cubs are less common and litters of three almost never occur in Alaska. Polar bear cubs have fur at birth, but weigh only one and a half pounds.

Newborn cubs are blind and helpless. When they emerge from the den in March or April, they will weigh 25 pounds and they may weigh as much as 200 pounds by their first birthday.

Polar bear families typically remain in the vicinity several days after emerging from the den. During this time the cubs romp and play and explore the outside world. This period of acclimation must be of great survival value since the female bears, which have not eaten since fall, extend the lengthy fast to provide for it. In Alaska, female bears usually breed for the first time at five years of age, producing cubs around their sixth year. Young bears remain with their mothers for two and a half years to learn how to hunt and survive on the ice. Therefore, litters are produced no more frequently than every third year. Some twenty-five to thirty year old bears have been captured in the wild, however most do not live beyond the age of twenty. Most females probably produce no more than five litters in a lifetime.

CURRENT STATUS AND THE FUTURE

Since the days of the Roman Empire polar bear furs have been prized and commercial exploitation has left an indelible mark on the current polar bear distribution. Local reductions in polar bear numbers have occurred in several parts of the world. Perhaps it is only the remoteness and unpredictability of the polar bear's habitat, and the inability of early man-made machines to traverse it, that saved the great white bears from extinction during the time of unregulated commercial hunting.

In recognition of the polar bear's increasing vulnerability to modern man's presence in the Arctic, the five nations within whose boundaries polar bears occur negotiated a conservation treaty in 1972. By virtue of this, the "International Agreement for the Conservation of Polar Bears," nations agreed to conduct national research programs designed to learn more about these creatures. They also agreed to regulate harvests within safe limits, to take measures protecting females and young, and to study and protect the ecosystems of which polar bears are a part.

There appears to be as many Alaskan polar bears today as there were in the 1950s. However, neither existing treaties nor our assessments afford wildlife managers much comfort. One reason is that our knowledge of polar bear is still rudimentary. Thus, our assessments could be in error. Also, compared to other species occupying the top of the food chain in other environments, polar bear populations appear naturally unstable. Dramatic fluctuations in bear numbers and conditions have been observed in response to periodic extremes in weather and ice. It may be that polar bears rarely approach the carrying capacity of their habitat. Rather, they are always reproducing as quickly as possible—which is not very fast—only to suffer periodic declines in their populations. Unregulated hunting, widespread Arctic development or any other disturbance that might aggravate natural population dynamics could be disastrous.

Finally, evidence suggests the Alaskan polar bear population is relatively small and widely dispersed. Off the coast of Alaska it takes about sixty square miles of ice habitat to support a single polar bear. Therefore, a small margin of safety surrounds any management decision which impacts polar bears or their habitat.

Harvests must be closely monitored and regulated within a sound management framework. Unfortunately, current federal legislation originally intended to promote conservation of marine mammals offers no mechanism for the protection of critical female segments of the population. In fact, this law prevents wildlife agencies from taking any management actions until the populations are determined to be depleted.

These management restrictions seem grave indeed in light of imminent developments in Alaska. Hydrocarbon exploration and production in the Arctic and the attendant human population increase could bring sweeping changes to portions of Alaskan polar bear habitat. Wildlife managers must possess the maximum flexibility to respond to natural or man-caused fluctuations in polar bear numbers. They must be willing and able to react in a positive manner to increased interest both in consumptive and non-consumptive uses of polar bears. And, they must be innovative if they are to simultaneously provide for mineral and energy development and allow the polar bear to remain the master of the northern ice.

COMMON GROUND

THIS IS THE SUN OF ARCTIC AUTUMN, low and heavy on the horizon. The darkness is returning, the cycle of cold and wind. It is autumn, the feel of the season hangs in the air like smoke. There is an emptiness that comes over Alaska in autumn. Everything seems to be packing up and moving out, the land emptying itself for winter. The sun slips to the horizon; salmon make their way upstream to spawn and die; strings of geese and ducks knit the storm skies into winter hues; long lines of caribou pull the snow behind them down the mountain slopes.

On the ridgeline behind camp there is a grizzly, silhouetted against the sun. Backlit, the bear seems to carry the last of the season's light in the rough edges of its fur. Soon, the long sleep.

Each autumn for a long line of autumns bears have denned up in the hillsides, under the windfalls and on the shore ice of Alaska. And, each spring for a long line of springs they have walked out into the sunshine of an Alaska changed little by the passing of a single season. But changes come more quickly now and each spring seems to bring change as rapidly as melting snow.

Alaska is teetered on the brink of change. Despite major cities like Anchorage and an oil pipeline 48-inches in diameter that cuts through the heart of the state for 789 miles, Alaska is still a blank page. Only one-twentieth of the state's land mass has been cleared, developed or altered directly by man's hand. But the hammer seems poised.

The Arctic National Wildlife Refuge in northeastern Alaska was established to preserve vital habitat for wildlife such as caribou, musk ox, bear and waterfowl. Yet, it sits atop an estimated 4.85 billion barrels of oil and 11.9 trillion cubic feet of natural gas. Studies done by the University of Alaska at Fairbanks have shown that even at distances as great as a half-mile, seismic testing has disturbed the metabollic rates of denned grizzlies, the kind of seismic testing done in oil and gas exploration.

Gates of the Arctic National Park and the contiguous Noatak National Preserve are kingdoms for grizzlies and black bears. Together they protect millions of acres of wildlife habitat and hundreds of miles of the wildest rivers left on this continent. Yet just across the Arctic Divide in the National Petroleum Reserve which is larger than the Park and Preserve combined, lies eighty percent of Alaska's coal reserves. Extending from the Arctic Divide north to the Arctic Ocean, development of these coal reserves could threaten polar bear habitat as well as grizzly and black bear country.

The Tongass National Forest in extreme southeastern Alaska was expanded by the 1980 passage of the Alaska National Interest Lands Conservation Act (ANILCA), a monumental act of Congress which added over 104 million acres of national parks, forests, refuges and monuments. Yet the same act mandated a timber harvest of 450 million board feet each year from the Tongass forest and already 385,000 acres have been logged damaging prime black bear habitat.

Another act of Congress with a long name, the Alaska Native Claims Settlement Act of 1971 (ANCSA) has also put the fate of millions of acres of bear country in the balance. The act granted over 44 million acres of land to 13 Native corporations around the state, land that was to be used to produce a profit for the corporations. Few of the corporations have yet shown a profit but in 1991 the currently Native-owned corporate stock will be opened for public sale, throwing yet another shadow on the future of a large part of Alaska and bear country.

Alaska seems to be walking the narrow ridge between development of its mineral and timber resources and preservation of its natural resources. It is a precarious walk. There will always be questions, debates over preservation or development. It will be up to us to provide the hard answers.

In some ways, many of the questions are already being answered. Places like McNeil River State Game Sanctuary where the bears and their habitat take precedence over tourists and treaties such as the one agreed to by all five Arctic nations with populations of polar bears and the Marine Mammals Protection Act are at least the first tentative steps towards finding solutions. Continued research efforts by the Alaska Department of Fish and Game and the United States Fish and Wildlife Service, as well as other scientific agencies and universities, are providing us with information on questions we may not yet even know how to ask.

Alaska is bear country, but human footprints have mingled with the tracks of polar bear, grizzly and black bear for over 12,000 years. It is common ground and the answers to the tough questions facing the state today will determine if Alaska is to remain a common ground.

Caught in the middle is the bear, backlit, carrying the last rays of autumn in its fur and restless with the ancient stirrings of the long winter sleep to come.

BIBLIOGRAPHY

Ashton, John, *Curious Creatures in Zoology,* John C. Nimmo, 1890

Behnke, Steven, "Subsistence Use of Brown Bear in Bristol Bay Area: A review of Available Information," Subsistence Division, Alaska Department of Fish and Game, March 1981

Bruemmer, Fred, *Encounters with Arctic Animals,* McGraw Hill–Ryerson Lmted., 1972

Carrighar, Sally, *Wild Heritage,* Houghton Mifflin Co., 1965

Collins, Henry B., Frederica de Laguna, Edmund Carpenter and Peter Stone, *The Far North: 2000 Years of American Eskimo and Indian Art,* Indiana University, 1977

Dufresne, Frank, *Alaska Animals and Fishes,* Binfords & Mort, 1946
   No Room for Bears, Holt, Rinehart and Winston, 1965

East, Ben, *Bears,* Outdoor Life, Crown Publishers, 1977

Field, Edward, *Eskimo Songs and Stories,* Delecorte Press, 1973

Ford, Barbara, *The Black Bear: The Spirit of the Wilderness,* Houghton Mifflin, 1981

Fruechun, Peter and Finn Salomonson, *The Arctic Year,* Putnam Co., 1958

Hall, Edwin, *The Eskimo Storyteller: Folktales from Noatak, Alaska,* University of Tennessee Press, 1975

Hallowell, A. Irving, "Bear Ceremonialism in the Northern Hemisphere," vol. 28, *American Anthropologist,* 1926

Harris, Leon, "Spirit World of the Bering Sea Eskimos" *Smithsonian* Magazine, May 1982

Haynes, Bessie Doak, and Edgar Haynes, *The Grizzly Bear: Portraits from Life,* University of Oklahoma Press, 1966

Herbert, Wally, *Eskimos,* Collins Publishers, 1976

Herrero, Stephan M., "Black Bears: The Grizzly's Replacement?", *The Black Bear in Modern North America,* Proceedings of the Workshop on the Management Biology of North American Black Bear, Feb. 1977
   "Aspects of Evolution and Adaption in American Black Bears *(Ursus americanus)* and Brown and Grizzly Bears *(Ursus arctos Linne)* of North America." *Bear—Their Biology and Management,* 2nd International Conference on Bear Research and Management, Nov. 1970

Holzworth, John M., *The Wild Grizzlies of Alaska,* G. Putnam's Sons, 1930

Kawagley, Dolores, *Yupik Stories,* Alaska Methodist University Press, 1975

Matthiessen, Peter, *Wildlife in America,* Viking Press, 1959

McCracken, Harold, *The Beast That Walks Like a Man: The Story of the Grizzly Bear,* Doubleday & Company, Inc. 1955

Mitchell, John G., "Last Stand of the Grizzly," *American Heritage,* October 1977

Morgan, Lael, *And the Land Provides: Alaskan Natives in a Year of Transition,* Anchor Press, Doubleday & Company, 1974

Murie, Olaus J., *A Field Guide to Animal Tracks,* Houghton Mifflin Company, 1974

Nelson, Richard K., *Hunters of the Northern Forest: Designs for Survival Among the Alaskan Kutchin,* University of Chicago Press, 1973
   Hunters of the Northern Ice, University of Chicago Press, 1969

Ormond, Clyde, *Bear!,* The Stackpole Company, 1961

Oswalt, Wendell H., *Alaskan Eskimos,* Chandler Publishing Co., 1967

Perry, Richard, *The Polar Worlds,* Taplinger Publishing Company, 1973
  The World of the Polar Bear, University of Washington Press, 1966

Ransom, Jay Ellis, Editor, *Complete Field Guide to North American Wildlife: Western Edition,* Harper and Row, 1981

Rausch, Robert L., "Geographic Variation in Size in North American Brown Bears, *Ursus arctos L.,* as indicated by Condylobasal Length," July 26, 1962

Ray, G. Carleton and M.G. McCormick-Ray, *Wildlife of the Polar Regions,* Chanticleer, 1981

Ray, Dorothy Jean, *Artists of the Tundra and the Sea,* University of Washington Press, 1961
  Eskimo Art: Traditions and Innovations in North Alaska, University of Washington Press, 1977
  Eskimo Masks: Arts and Ceremony, University of Washington Press, 1967

Reynolds, Harry V., "North Slope Grizzly Bear Studies." Alaska Department of Fish and Game, May 1980

Rooth, Anna Birgitta, *The Alaskan Expedition: Myths, Customs and Beliefs among the Athabascan Indians and Eskimos of Northern Alaska,* Lund, 1971

Schneider, William, *Where the Grizzly Walks,* Montana Press Publishing Co., 1977

Sherwood, Morgan, *Big Game in Alaska: A History of Wildlife and People,* Yale University Press, 1981

Smith, Kaj Birket, and Frederica de Laguna, *Eyak Indians of the Copper River Delta Alaska,* Denmark, 1938

South, Malcom, Editor, *Topsell's History of Beasts,* Nelson–Hall, 1981

Spencer, Robert F., *The North Alaskan Eskimo: A Study in Ecology and Society,* Dover, 1959

Stefansson, Vilhjalmur, *My Life with the Eskimos,* MacMillan Company, 1913

Thwaites, Reuben, Editor, *The Original Journals of the Lewis and Clark Expedition 1804-1806,* Dodd, Mead and Company, Inc., 1921

Wells, James K., *Ipani Eskimos: A Cycle of Life in Nature,* Alaskan Methodist University Press, 1974

Wherry, Joseph H., *The Totem Pole Indians,* Thomas Cromwell Co., Inc., 1974

Weyer, Edward Moffat, *The Eskimos: Their Environment and Folkways,* Anchor Books, Yale Unviersity Press, 1969

Wood, Gerald L., *Animal Facts and Feats,* Sterling Publishing Co., 1977

ACKNOWLEDGMENTS

This book has traveled a long, winding path, and there are many people to thank: Tom Beck for the days spent tracking bears and the nights spent talking about bears, Chuck Schwartz for the field time and the moose steak, Harry Reynolds, Steve Amstrup, Dennis Branham, Will Troyer, Dr. Fred Dean, Sterling Miller, Dr. Erich Follmann, John Heckel, Jill Wolf-Reinicke for the days apart while I researched the book and for worrying, and Rick Rinehart for support of the project. Finally, I would like to thank Christina Watkins for that rare combination of grace and strength it takes to see a work like this through to the end.

—J.R.

CHRISTINA WATKINS, the designer and producer of *Bears of Alaska in Life and Legend*, would like to express her gratitude to John Domont, George Huey, Barry Lopez, Bob Petersen, Jeff Rennicke, Carry Rezabeck, Rick Rinehart, and Gary Snyder for their support and continuing belief in the importance of this book.

PHOTOGRAPHIC CREDITS

Steven C. Amstrup, pages 45, 53
Tom Beck, page 24
Thor Larsen, page 48
Torgeir Lekang Leeson, pages 12 & 21
Steve McCutcheon, pages 9 & 15
Rick McIntyre, pages 5, 8, 28, 36, 61, & back cover
Harry Reynolds, cover
Will Troyer, pages 25 & 40

Artifacts on pages 37 & 49 courtesy of the Taylor Museum Collection, Colorado Springs Fine Arts Center.

All smaller illustrations by Pam Lungé.

Illustration page 13, *Tuwa Tuli*, stonecut by Pitu, 1961, Dorset Eskimo Cooperative.